75 Down Blocks

Also by Rick Clark

Pressure Point Fighting: A Guide to the Secret Heart of Asian Martial Arts

75 Down Blocks

REFINING KARATE TECHNIQUE

Rick Clark

Tuttle Publishing
Boston ■ Rutland, VT ■ Tokyo

Please note that the author and publisher of this book are NOT RESPONSIBLE in any manner whatsoever for any injury that may result from practicing the techniques and/or following the instructions given within. Since the physical activities described herein may be too strenuous in nature for some readers to engage in safely, it is essential that a physician be consulted prior to training.

First published in 2003 by Tuttle Publishing, an imprint of Periplus Editions (HK) Ltd., with editorial offices at 153 Milk Street, Boston, Massachusetts 02109.

Copyright © 2003 Rick Clark

All rights reserved. No part of this publication may be reproduced or utilized in any form or by any means, electronic or mechanical, including photocopying, recording, or by any information storage and retrieval system, without prior written permission from Tuttle Publishing.

Library of Congress Cataloging-in-Publication Data
Clark, Rick, 1948-
  75 down blocks : refining karate technique / Rick Clark.
    p.cm.
  Includes bibliographical references.
  ISBN 0-8048-3218-8 (pbk.)
  I. Karate. I. Title: Seventy-five down blocks. II. Title

GV1114.3 .G515 2003
796.815'3--dc21   2002075064

Distributed by

North America, Latin America, and Europe
Tuttle Publishing
Distribution Center
Airport Industrial Park
364 Innovation Drive
North Clarendon, VT 05759-9436
Tel: (802) 773-8930
Fax: (802) 773-6993
Email: info@tuttlepublishing.com

Asia Pacific
Berkeley Books Pte. Ltd.
130 Joo Seng Road
#06-01/03 Olivine Building
Singapore 368357
Tel: (65) 6280-3220
Fax: (65) 6280-6290
Email: inquiries@periplus.com.sg

Japan
Tuttle Publishing
Yaekari Bldg., 3F
5-4-12 Ōsaki, Shinagawa-ku
Tokyo 141-0032
Tel: 81-35-437-0171
Fax: 81-35-437-0755
Email: tuttle-sales@gol.com

First edition
08 07 06 05 04 03   9 8 7 6 5 4 3 2 1

Design by Stephanie Doyle
Printed in the United States of America

Contents

Preface	ix
PART ONE	1
Chapter One: The Evolution of the Martial Arts	2
Chapter Two: Pareto's Law and the Martial Artist	12
Chapter Three: Taking the Initiative	22
PART TWO: Down Blocks	29
Chapter Four: Defense Against a Kick	32
Technique 1	33
Technique 2	34
Technique 3	36
Technique 4	39
Chapter Five: Defense Against a Same-Side Wrist Grab	41
Technique 5	42
Technique 6	43
Technique 7	46
Technique 8	48
Technique 9	50
Technique 10	52
Technique 11	55
Chapter Six: Defense Against a Cross-Hand Wrist Grab	57
Technique 12	58
Technique 13	60
Technique 14	62
Technique 15	63
Technique 16	64
Technique 17	66
Technique 18	67
Chapter Seven: Defense Against a Double-Wrist Grab	70
Technique 19	71
Technique 20	72

Technique 21	74
Technique 22	75
Technique 23	77
Technique 24	79
Technique 25	80
Chapter Eight: Defense Against an Upper-Arm Grab	82
Technique 26	83
Technique 27	85
Technique 28	86
Technique 29	88
Technique 30	90
Chapter Nine: Preemptive Techniques	92
Technique 31	93
Technique 32	94
Technique 33	96
Technique 34	98
Technique 35	99
Technique 36	100
Technique 37	102
Chapter Ten: Defense Against a Push	105
Technique 38	106
Technique 39	107
Technique 40	108
Technique 41	110
Technique 42	111
Technique 43	113
Technique 44	114
Technique 45	116
Chapter Eleven: Defense Against a Single-Hand Lapel Grab	118
Technique 46	119
Technique 47	120
Technique 48	121
Technique 49	123
Technique 50	124
Technique 51	126

Chapter Twelve: Defense Against a Double-Hand Grab to the Upper Body	128
Technique 52	129
Technique 53	130
Technique 54	132
Technique 55	133
Technique 56	135
Chapter Thirteen: Defense Against a Grab from the Rear	137
Technique 57	138
Technique 58	139
Technique 59	141
Technique 60	142
Technique 61	144
Technique 62	146
Technique 63	147
Technique 64	149
Chapter Fourteen: Defense Against a Punch	151
Technique 65	152
Technique 66	153
Technique 67	154
Technique 68	156
Chapter Fifteen: Defense Against a Stick	158
Technique 69	159
Technique 70	160
Technique 71	162
Technique 72	164
Technique 73	165
Technique 74	167
Technique 75	168
Appendix A: Pressure Points	171
Appendix B: Erwin Von Baelz and the Revival of the Japanese Martial Arts	173
Bibliography	183

Preface

Silla, stuhl, sedia, cadeira, and chaise. What do all of these words have in common? They are five words that all translate to the English word "chair." If I were to ask the individuals who spoke these languages to draw a picture of what that word represented, they would all draw a picture of the same object. Would the objects they draw all look exactly the same? Probably not, but there would be enough of a similarity between each of the five pictures that all of the drawings would represent a chair.

Even if I were to ask you to stop for a moment and picture a "chair" in your mind, I would be willing to bet the chair you are thinking of is not the same as the chair I am thinking of as I write this paragraph. Each of us has a vision of a chair in our mind, and each of these visions is a true representation of a metaphysical idea.

When we use the term silla, stuhl, sedia, cadeira, chaise, or any other word meaning chair, it represents an archetypal chair—or all of the possible variations of a chair. Thus, the way we visualize what a chair *is* is based on our previous life experiences. Or, to go one step further, the chair you are sitting on now is simply a real version of all the possible chairs.

So far this has not taken us very far into the realm of the martial arts. But here's where the fun comes in. Instead of thinking of a chair, think of a "down block." Each style of karate, tae kwon do, kung fu, or other similar martial art has this movement in its *kata* (forms). Just as there are hundreds of types of real chairs, there are also hundreds of different types of down blocks. Each down block shares enough similar characteristics with other down blocks to be recognized as a down block by other martial artists, even though it may not be the same kind of down block they use. Just as not everyone in the world sits in the same chair, down blocks are different for each style or system.

In this book I want to go one step beyond the average down block and explore the range of possible down blocks. Just as you cannot say that any one chair is the only real chair, it is equally impossible for a person to say any particular down block is the only true *bunkai* (interpretation of kata). There are, in my opinion, many different applications for the down block, and each application requires an adaptation before it becomes an ideal bunkai for each individual or situation.

This book offers seventy-five possible explanations of the down block. By concentrating on one of the most common movements found in the various kata in this kind of detail, and offering various applications for the technique, we can improve the overall practice and understanding of martial arts.

For this book, I have taken common attacks and applied the down block movement in self-defensive situations. The variations shown may appear to be similar, but if you look closely, you will notice that they are in fact different techniques.

Part 1 of the book offers examples of my approach, which consists of focusing on the details of basic concepts or techniques to get at the invaluable complexity and subtlety that lie beneath them.

The techniques in Part 2 of this book have been divided into twelve broad sections. Because this book was designed to cover only seventy-five techniques, there are limitations to the number of attacks discussed. Each chapter contains bunkai for the down block in four to eight scenarios. They include:

1. Defense against a kick
2. Defense against a same-side wrist grab
3. Defense against a cross-hand wrist grab
4. Defense against a double-wrist grab
5. Defense against an upper-arm grab
6. Preemptive techniques
7. Defense against a push
8. Defense against a single-hand lapel grab
9. Defense against a double-hand grab to the upper body
10. Defense against a grab from the rear
11. Defense against a punch
12. Defense against a stick

It is my hope that this book will give you a starting point, where you can begin to see applications for the down block in terms that meet your level of experience and need.

—*Rick Clark*

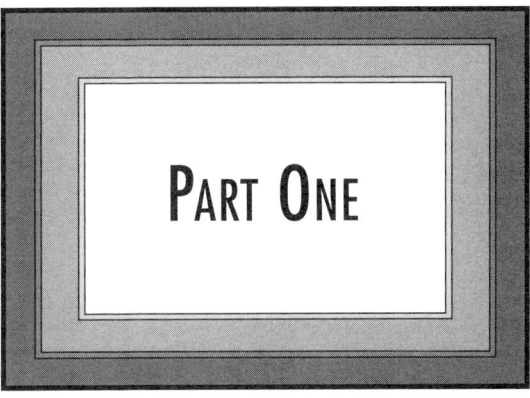

The Evolution of the Martial Arts

Grasping the essence of karate-do is an elusive goal reached only by few. If we understand that the kata were designed as a method for remembering self-defense techniques, it is easy to understand what Funakoshi (1975) means when he states, "if you merely move your hands and feet and jump up and down like a puppet, learning karate is not very different from learning to dance. You will never have reached the heart of the matter, you will have failed to grasp the quintessence of Karate-do" (p. 104).

Funakoshi held fast to the principle that the true secrets of karate were to be found in the various kata. He (1988) states, "Looking over the thirty-odd kata, he [a student] should be able to see that they are essentially variations on just a handful. If you truly understand a single technique, you need only observe the forms and be told the essential points of the others" (p. 44).

In the words of one of Funakoshi's early students Shigero Egami (1976), speaking of the "*Yoi*" or ready posture, he states, "I know that there are changes in function among the various kata, but I must confess that I do not know the reason, nor why they change according to the kata" (p. 107). If a senior student of Funakoshi did not fully understand kata, how can we expect to "truly understand" them?

The Bunkai of the Down Block

The down block is perhaps the most common technique used in martial arts. The "down block" motion is found in virtually all kata and is utilized in various stances.

Though used in every school, the basic motion is the same regardless of the system: One hand comes up toward the opposite side of the head then moves down to groin level, while the opposite hand is brought back to one's side. The exact placement of both hands will vary slightly, but this is a minor factor as such discrepancies can be found even within an individual system.

The inclusion of this movement in so many kata is a clear indication of how important this movement must have been in the eyes of the old masters.

When we understand that studying kata is the key to understanding martial arts, we realize that by practicing bunkai of the down block, and developing the technique to its fullest, we can deepen our understanding of the martial art that we study, and in the process strengthen our own practice.

Unfortunately, this can be a frustrating process. Often we don't know why we are taught specific bunkai. And without a deep understanding of our martial art, we are unable to develop our own bunkai. Instructors teach and practice exact positioning to meet their particular interpretation of the kata. But when questioned why such positions are practiced or why small changes are made in the kata, a typical response is "we have been researching the movement and feel this is a better position to have your hand."

Often, that is the full extent of the explanation.

So, why are we taught such simplistic bunkai if kata are so important to our understanding of martial arts? When I began to look at explanations for the various movements in the kata, I became very interested in the answer to this question. I began looking into the history of the martial arts and, in doing so, I discovered a number of reasons why we have been taught this way.

If we look at the history of martial arts, we find a number of developments that help explain this:

- Knowledge of the more esoteric aspects of the martial arts has been kept secret from the general population, so that those in the upper ranks can maintain their position of authority.
- Historical developments in Japan—specifically, the Western "opening" of Japan in the mid-nineteenth century—made it necessary for the nation to move beyond the martial arts as part of its military culture.

- When combat techniques, which had been restricted to the warrior class, began to be taught to the general public, they were often modified to be less dangerous—or less effective, depending on how you look at it.
- These techniques were further simplified when the martial arts were introduced into school systems as a form of discipline or fitness training.

As a result, the esoteric aspects of martial arts slowly became less and less visible—and the simpler, more formalized aspects of the martial arts forms began to dominate.

Maintaining Authority

History is replete with examples of those in power attempting to maintain their power by restricting access to weapons or knowledge. This veil of secrecy is found throughout the martial arts. In feudal Japan, only the warrior class (*bushi*) were allowed to carry two swords.

Bujutsu was considered to be the exclusive domain of the warrior class. "Commoners, while not totally without weapons, nevertheless were forbidden to possess the types used by the bushi and were refused permission to study the bujutsu"(Drager 1983 p. 53).

Early writers on the martial arts have described how secretive instructors were about keeping knowledge of *the martial arts* from the general public. Koyama & Minami (1913), for example, state, "the knowledge of jiu jitsu [sic] has only recently been made general in Japan" (p. 6). The "upper classes, jealous lest their influence over the populace should wane, tried to keep it to themselves" (Ibid., p. 6).

Funakoshi stated that karate as taught in Japan was "not the same karate that was practiced even as recently as ten years ago, and it is a long way indeed from the karate that I learned when I was a child in Okinawa" (Funakoshi 1975, p. 36).

It was not uncommon for martial arts teachers to teach only a small number of their students the real secrets of a system. We can assume that Funakoshi did not teach a deep understanding of kata to his beginning students. The "martial arts masters of old would confer a diploma and reveal key elements only to those disciples whose training, almost unbearably hard and austere, had lead them to experience directly the spirit of budo"(Ibid., p. 44).

Aikido masters, for example, have been taught groups of techniques known as *kaeshi-waza*. Kaeshi-waza are techniques that involve a blending from one movement to another, which will allow the initiated to emerge victorious over their opponent. Saito (1974) offers an illuminating discussion of kaeshi-waza that are handed down to high-rank black belts in aikido:

"In olden days, Founder Morihei Ueshiba used to initiate his leading disciples into the art of kaeshi-waza prior to sending them out in the world as undefeatable instructors. The instructors, armed with kaeshi-waza, were thus able to gain leadership always in their training sessions even when they were in a defensive position" (p. 125).

It is clear that Ueshiba went so far as to withhold secret techniques from the lower-rank Japanese students to maintain the superiority of his upper-rank students.

Jujitsu practitioners regarded the strikes to vital points of the body as secret techniques and would not impart this knowledge to novices. The master of a system would only teach the full system to the individual who would be the "inheritor of his entire method" (Yamanaka 1918, p. 208).

Some of this caution was understandable, given the circumstances.

For example, if you were an instructor who knew deadly techniques, would you teach these secrets to those who had recently conquered your nation? Probably not. Okinawa was a conquered nation, ruled by the Japanese. How likely is it that Funakoshi ever revealed the true secrets of karate-do to his senior Japanese students? To use another, more current example, how likely is it that American servicemen would be taught the real meaning of karate after W.W. II?

Sometimes the barriers ran along national or ethnic lines.

For example, the development of kyusho-jitsu or atemi-waza in the Japanese martial arts "lagged behind the more advanced systems of China and the Chinese-influenced fighting systems of Korea and Okinawa" (Drager 1973, p. 134). With the transmission of Okinawan karate to the mainland of Japan during the Taisho era (1912–26), it is likely that Gichin Funakoshi did not teach kyusho-jitsu to the general population. (It is also possible he did not teach the advanced techniques to his senior students.)

Koyama & Minami (1913) state, "There are some jiu jitsu [sic] maneuvers that have never been explained to Europeans or Americans—and probably they never will be.

"These death blows are remarkable. Some are delivered on the spine, others on the neck and head, and two on the face. There are almost numberless maneuvers that temporarily paralyze nerves and nerve centers, and others that stop the circulation of the blood in various parts of the body"(pp. 5–6).

Vairamuttu (1954, p. 21) shares their conviction: "Whether the real secrets of advanced jujitsu, which are so greatly treasured by the Japanese and imparted under vow of strict secrecy to pupils of unquestionable moral character, have ever been divulged to Occidentals, is very much open to doubt."

The "real secrets" to which Vairamuttu referred, of course, were the methods of attacking the vital points of the body, and resuscitation after the administration of such blows. Ueshiba, then, it appears, went one step further and purposely withheld techniques from any student who was not Japanese. This statement is supported by Stevens' (1987) quotation from Morihei Ueshiba's privately circulated text *Budo*, published in 1938, which gives the warning "This manual is not to be shown to non-Japanese" (p. 78).

BUDO VS. JUTSU

The evolution of the martial arts from combat techniques to a spiritual discipline for the general public also affected the way the arts were taught.

Kendo is one example of how bujutsu techniques were transformed into a form of budo—as early as the beginning of the seventeenth century.

With this development, "the essence of kendo was stated at that time to be more spiritual discipline for the improvement of personal character than an activity directly concerned with combat" (Drager 1975, p. 68). Originally designed for life-and-death situations, kendo now looked to the spiritual perfection of the individual. This shift in emphasis to the noncombative aspect was "the first time that swordsmanship in any form had been openly offered as available to all classes of people" (Ibid., p. 68).

This division exists across the whole range of traditional martial arts styles. It is quite clear, for example, that there is a difference between arts such as kenjutsu and kendo, or ju-jutsu and judo.

Each approach has its advocates and its critics. Drager (1974), for example, notes that, to "traditionalists and to those who regard classical bujutsu from the viewpoint of actual combat, the modern disciplines are nothing but an ass in a tiger's skin" (p. 55).

Another way of looking at these two ways of approaching martial arts training is to say that one treats martial arts as a "sport," while the other represents "self-defense."

You can also differentiate the two major groupings as "do" or "jutsu." Of course, this is a very simplistic way of describing the difference. Nor are these hard and fast divisions, since a martial art system that promotes the sport or physical fitness aspects can be used in a self-defense situation. Likewise, an art that promotes self-defense as a primary concern can have aspects of sport and physical fitness.

There are as many variations on these two broad categories as there are instructors. I especially do not want to place any value judgment on the value or worth of any one system, or orientation. Each is valuable and serves the purpose of the individual. This is, of course, the way it should be.

How did these different approaches develop?

One of the primary influences was historical. Prior to the Meiji restoration in the late nineteenth century the martial arts represented an important part of Japan's combat effectiveness. Once Japan was confronted with the military advances of the Western powers, its rulers quickly realized that their feudal warfare techniques, which relied on the samurai, were no longer practical. It became all too clear that the traditional way was not a viable approach to the defense of the nation.

Japan recognized that it needed to create a modern army and navy—along with the infrastructure to support the modernization of the nation—to survive its encounter with the West. As Japan began to modernize its military forces, the traditional martial arts were left behind, and new institutions were built based on the most up-to-date and successful models of the time. Japan based its navy on that of Great Britain and its army on the German model—each the dominant power in those fields at the time.

It may be impossible for us to imagine what a revolution this would have been in the worldview of the Japanese. Much of what they knew about the world—and their role in it—was turned upside down in an instant. Try to imagine what it would be like if our country found out we were 50 to 100 years behind the rest of the world in technology! We'd have to discard many of our old assumptions and institutions, and race to adopt new ways of thinking and doing things, just to catch up.

It was during this time that the martial arts of Japan began to divide into the two separate approaches described above.

Teachers began to develop the modern budo forms of aikido and judo—not as a form of combat, but for spiritual and physical development. Aikido and judo came from similar backgrounds, that is, jujitsu. Judo, the older of the two styles, was systematized in 1882 by Jigoro Kano. In 1925, Morihei Ueshiba organized aikido, which was then known as aiki-jujuts.

Both men modified the older systems of jujitsu to create newer styles, which "in the main [are] unrelated to real combat" (Drager 1973, p. 138). Kano was quite open in his acknowledgement that he removed the dangerous techniques from the syllabus of judo. In fact, judo relegated the practice of *kyusho* (striking vital points of the body) to kata (Koizumi 1967) so that it was not necessary to strike these points on an opponent.

The modern discipline of judo was at the forefront of this change. *Judoka* trained to improve their physical fitness and mental health. Judo had proved itself as a practical self-defense system through victories by its members in contests against other schools of jujitsu. It must be remembered that many of the early senior members of the *kodokan* had been trained in jujitsu systems.

Judo quickly became the dominant modern martial arts discipline, and as such many of its practices were copied by others.

For example, Gichin Funakoshi introduced karate into Japan in 1922. As karate's proponents tried to gain recognition for it as a martial art, they realized that it was necessary to have a standard training uniform. The *karate-ka* of the time developed a lighter version of the *judo-gi* as their standard training outfit. In much the same way, judo's belt system (*kyu/dan*[1]) was adopted to meet the needs of the emerging karate-ka.

The widespread adoption of the kyu/dan system is a clear indication of Jigoro Kano's open-minded adaptability. In the seventeenth century, Dosaku (1645–1702), a grand master of the board game Go, introduced the kyu/dan system as a method of handicapping the game.

Professor Kano is credited with introducing the kyu/dan system in the martial arts, but his was an act of "appropriation," not an original contribution to Japanese culture. It is evident that Professor Kano was willing to look outside of the traditional martial arts practices to find ideas that could be applied to his new "art" of judo. His willingness to adapt new ways of thinking and training from other disciplines was critical to the development of the contemporary martial arts.

Martial Arts in the School System

If you knew how to teach your students how to knock out their opponents by lightly striking specific parts of the body, would you be willing to share that knowledge with every high-school student in your city? Of course not! This kind of powerful technique should be withheld from all but a very few of an instructor's best students.

I am firmly convinced that the major reason that the knowledge of the bunkai has declined is the growing influence of sport and physical education approaches to the martial arts.

The leading force in the adaptation of traditional martial arts was Professor Jigoro Kano and his promulgation of judo.[2]

Please understand I am not disparaging judo—or Kano—in any way. What Professor Kano did for traditional Japanese martial arts was extremely important and provided invaluable leadership for those who followed in his footsteps. Without his active role in the martial arts, the various martial arts would not have the great popularity they do throughout the world.

Judo, and through its influence the other martial arts, introduced the general public to techniques that absolutely had to be modified for safety. Rules were required so that individuals could engage in contests. Yes, you could have had full-contact matches, but this would have limited judo to a small, select audience. In order to introduce judo into the school system, it was crucial that safety measures be put in place to protect the participants from harm.

Just as Kano developed judo so that the dangerous techniques were removed, allowing judo to be taught in the school system of Japan, it appears that Funakoshi also taught karate in such a way as to be appropriate for the school system. As he states, "Hoping to see karate included in the universal physical education taught in our public schools, I set about revising the kata so as to make them as simple as possible"(Ibid., p. 36).

The beginning of the simplification of kata, however, can be credited to one of Funakoshi's teachers, Anko Itosu. In the early 1900s, he developed the five Pinan kata that were then taught in the Okinawan school system. "An alert military doctor noticed the physical condition of Okinawan conscripts, which was attributed to the practice of *Te*. Karate was then included in the physical education curriculum in 1903" (Drager 1973, p. 59). This was of course prior to the introduction of karate into Japan in 1922.

With the transmission of martial arts teaching into the school system, forms became greatly simplified. Far from their original "roots" in combat and self-defense, the martial arts were presented as healthy and spiritual. This successful adaptation, developed by Kano, has been followed by succeeding martial arts instructors, even to this day.

The Role of the Down Block

To answer the more general question, it should be clear that this historical "demilitarization" of the martial arts has led to a significant simplification in the techniques that we are taught.

Since the late 1980s, there has been a movement to research and rediscover how vital points—one of the aspects that has been "left out" of most contemporary martial arts training—were utilized in the various martial arts. This has brought about a more general resurgence in the study of kata (forms) and the various possible applications.

The main purpose of this book is to show you how to expand your base of knowledge of the martial arts. By looking at the technique of the down block in such great detail, I hope to show you something of the original depth, flexibility and power of the technique—before it was systematized into modern teaching methods.

Hopefully, this close examination will help you develop a deeper appreciation for and understanding of the effective self-defense practices that lie behind the more formal sets of movements that make up the training.

Please note that I'm not advocating that you question the training offered by your teachers. Practice the techniques as taught and teach the techniques as taught. Many times you will not understand the importance of a technique until you've practiced it for years.

What I do suggest is that you look at the techniques you're learning with a more critical eye. Does the technique work? How effective is it? Why are we changing the movements of a kata? How does this small change affect the bunkai of the kata? Is the bunkai of the kata now different from before? How does this improve the effectiveness of the movement?

You can learn as much from paying attention to the results of every variation, every small change, as you can from perfecting a given movement. Each variation, and its effect, adds a new dimension to your understanding of the technique.

This collection of bunkai of the down block is my contribution to the resurgence of interest in the original complexity and power of the martial arts. It represents my attempt to become better acquainted with kata and to gain a deeper understanding of bunkai in self-defense.

If you looked at the various movements found in karate, you would find certain groups of techniques that are repeated over and over again. Each system has a core group of techniques that embody the art. One such technique is the down block with its variations seen in the various systems of martial arts. For this book, I have taken common attacks and applied the down block movement in self-defensive situations.

Notes

1. The kyu/dan system is a method of ranking individuals. The lowest grade is tenth kyu, with the highest kyu grade being first kyu. Dan grades are higher than the kyu grades, and they start with first dan, with tenth being the highest grade.
2. The story of how the martial arts in Japan were transformed from combat skills into forms that emphasized health and fitness is one of the most fascinating chapters in the history of contemporary martial arts. For a quick look at one aspect of it, check out Appendix B.

Pareto's Law and the Martial Artist

Pareto's 80/20 law is a statistical discovery that I think has considerable relevance in the study of the martial arts. In brief, over 100 years ago, Vilfredo Pareto discovered a relationship that manifests itself repeatedly in larger systems.

In its most basic form, Pareto's 80/20 law states that you will get 80 percent of your results from 20 percent of your effort. In the business world, for example, it implies that you'll get 80 percent of your business from 20 percent of your customers. In the academic world, it implies that you'll probably get 80 percent of your research results from 20 percent of your time spent in the library, or 20 percent of your fieldwork.

When you first encounter this 80/20 rule, you may get the mistaken idea that the ratio between effort and results should be exactly 80/20. This is not really the case; the actual percentages vary from case to case. Rather, this ratio should be thought of as a guide, designed to remind you of the disproportionate effect of effort compared to results.

As you begin to recognize the 80/20 patterns that exist around you, the application of Pareto's rule will become apparent in everyday situations—in personal relationships, financial dealings, and national and international events.

In this chapter, I hope to demonstrate a few ways in which you can use the 80/20 rule to help you analyze and improve your martial arts training.

Why Do You Study the Martial Arts?

One immediate application of the 80/20 rule covers the motivation of individuals who begin taking martial arts classes. Over the years that I have been involved in the martial arts, I have been curious as to why individuals begin their training. I have also posed this question to many instructors. While I haven't conducted a scientific survey on the issue, I am reasonably confident in my conclusions—that out of all of the good reasons why someone would start to study the martial arts, most people begin for the purpose of self-defense. In other words, self-defense, which is just a small part of the range of possible reasons, is the primary motivation for the vast majority of individuals who take up the martial arts.

There's a sharp contrast between this perceived need for self-defense skills and the actual incidence of violent crime. For example, if we look at the risk of violence to an individual, it is extremely low. Mattinson (2001) noted that only 3 percent of the adult population of the United Kingdom was a victim of stranger and/or acquaintance violence in 1999. (Of course crime rates will vary from country to country, but I would guess that the statistics are relatively consistent in countries that are economically and culturally similar.)

I would guess that if we had asked prospective students—especially those interested in studying the martial arts for self-defense—what percentage of adults were likely to be a victim of a violent attack, they would have responded with a much higher number.

This type of information can serve as a bit of a reality check. Remember, only 3 percent of adults were victims of violent attack. Another way to look at this is that only 3 percent of the population had any real need for self-defense, while the other 97 percent didn't really need self-defense training. Here we have an example of Pareto's law—in reverse! Out of the large percentage of martial arts students motivated by their perceived need for self-defense, only a very few will actually have to deal with violent crimes.

In general, the more you know about the incidence of violent crime, the more likely that you'll be able to avoid it. For example, 7 out of 10 violent incidents occurred during the evening or night. To be even more specific, half of the incidents occurred between 6 P.M. Friday evening and 6 A.M. Monday morning. Another way to look at this would be that 70 percent of the violent assaults occurred during the evening or night. More than 50 percent of the assaults occurred during only 3 of the 7 days of the week. Clearly, if you want to reduce the likelihood that you'll become a victim of a violent assault, you should exercise greater caution during these times.

Developing a Plan of Attack

The rule also comes in handy for planning what facets of a martial arts system to study or emphasize—especially if your primary motivation is self-defense. If you look at the complete range of ways you can be attacked, it seems infinite—which makes planning a defense very difficult. Yet, if you stop to look at the statistics behind this assumption, it turns out that there are a limited number of ways in which you are likely to be attacked.

In other words, out of a large number of potential attacks, you are really only likely to encounter a limited number of techniques. If your primary concern is to learn or teach self-defense, you can use this knowledge to determine what kinds of attacks you should concentrate on during practice. This allows you to devote a larger portion of your training time to practicing against attacks you might reasonably expect to encounter. To put it in terms of Pareto's law—80 percent of the attacks will be based on 20 percent of the possible attacking techniques. And it makes sense that 80 percent (more or less) of our training time would be spent practicing defenses against that 20 percent.

It's generally accepted that law enforcement officers face more situations requiring skills in self-defense than the average individual. Law enforcement is one of a small number of occupations that subject an individual to greater than average chances of being a victim of a violent assault. If you are a taxi driver, convenience store clerk, bartender, or bouncer you can also expect to be at greater risk. I've chosen to use statistics describing attacks on law enforcement personnel for several reasons, the major one being that, in today's world, government agencies have collected and compiled data that is readily available.

If you look at the data describing the methods used to assault law enforcement officers, you may be able to generalize (with great care) as to how likely an individual in the larger population is to be assaulted—and, therefore, which techniques to emphasize in your training.

The Federal Bureau of Investigation (FBI) has collected much of the information needed for such research. I have reproduced a very small amount of their data from *Law Enforcement Officers Killed and Assaulted* (1978–2000). Data has been summarized to give a total of the number of law enforcement officers (LEO) killed or assaulted in the United States. It is clear that law enforcement officers are more often assaulted with personal weapons—fist, hand, foot, elbow, knee, and so on—than any other weapon (82.73 percent). From these statistics, it is clear the 80/20 rule operates in this context—out of the broad range of possible attacks, a small number of techniques are used in the great majority of incidents.

Federal Bureau of Investigation Law Enforcement Officers Killed and Assaulted 1978–2000

Total Law Enforcement Officers Assaulted	1,278,987	100%
Personal Weapons (hands, feet, elbow etc.)	1,057,959	82.72%
Other Dangerous Weapons	126,624	9.90%
Firearms	62,498	4.89%
Knives or Cutting Instruments	31,906	2.49%

If you are going to design a program to teach law enforcement officers self-defense techniques, it is obvious that it's very important to teach skills that correspond to the actual needs of the officers. Given the number of attacks involving "personal weapons" (hands, feet, and so on), close-quarter combat techniques designed to meet an empty-handed attacker should play a dominant role in any such training program.

Consider that when suspects apply some type of weaponless tactic against a law enforcement officer they do so with the full knowledge that the officer is armed with a firearm. It would also seem logical that the suspects would attack the officers most often with percussive techniques (punching, kicking, and so on) in an effort to disable the officer as quickly as possible. Yet just the opposite is true: 73.29 percent of the time an officer was grabbed in some manner, as compared to 13.65 percent of the time when an attacker resorted to a percussive technique. Surprising information, but invaluable if you're planning on training for self-defense.

The following chart details the unarmed tactics used when law enforcement officers are attacked.

Suspects' Use of Weaponless Tactics in 7,512 Arrests

	Arrests	Percent of Arrests
No Tactics Used	7,100	94.5154%
At Least One Tactic Used	412	5.4846%
All Arrests	7,512	100.00%
Type of Tactic:		
Spit	74	7.2125%
Grab	114	11.1111%
Twist Arm	128	12.4756%
Wrestle	262	25.5361%
Push/Shove	166	16.1793%
Hit	66	6.4327%
Kick	74	7.2125%
Bite/Scratch	39	3.8012%
Pressure Hold	16	1.5595%
Carotid Hold	12	1.1696%
Control Hold	21	2.047%
Other Tactic	54	5.2632%
Number of Tactics	1,026	13.66%

Tactic Where Suspect Grabbed, Pushed, or Shoved

Grab	114	15.160%
Twist Arm	128	17.021%
Wrestle	262	34.840%
Push/Shove	166	22.074%
Pressure Hold	16	2.128%
Carotid Hold	12	1.596%
Control Hold	54	5.2632%
Total	752	*100%*

	Percussive Tactic Used	
Hit	66	47.143%
Kick	74	52.857%
Total	*140*	*100%*

*Since some arrests involve the use of more than one tactic, the percentages under type of tactics do not add up to 100 percent. Taken from "Use of Force by Police: Overview of National and Local Data," p. 34, October 1999, National Institute of Justice.

From this data, we see that the unarmed assaults officers experience most commonly are: spit, grab, arm twist, wrestle, push/shove, hit, kick, bite/scratch, pressure hold, carotid hold (choke), control hold, or other tactic. To summarize the data for ease of use, we can say that there are four main types of attacks that one would be most likely to encounter in a self-defense situation. They are:

1. A grab
2. A push
3. A punch
4. A kick

It seems likely that these are the kinds of attacks, probably used in combinations, which you will be confronted with, if you need to defend yourself. This information is invaluable if you study the martial arts for self-defense. Each of these four groups of techniques can be analyzed so that you can develop effective self-defense techniques.

For example, if you look at a grab, there are only a few ways that an individual can commonly grab you. They are:

1. A same-side grab, where an opponent grabs your left side with his right hand
2. A cross-hand grab, where an opponent grabs your right side with his right hand
3. A two-handed grab

Breaking this down even further, the location of the grab will probably be your:

1. Wrist
2. Forearm

3. Upper arm
4. Lapel
5. Throat

Of course, there are other ways to grab someone—you may find yourself being grabbed by the leg or ankle. But in the normal situations this would be somewhat unlikely.

If you look at kicks, it would seem to me that you would most likely be attacked with a variation of a front kick, since the front kick is the most natural kick we practice. Roundhouse and side kicks could be encountered, but a jump spinning reverse side kick would have to rank very low on kicks one could expect to encounter.

Could you encounter this kind of attack? Of course—there are enough people today who have taken martial arts lessons to have a working knowledge of this type of kick, and there are enough people who have watched martial arts movies to perhaps try this kick. But once again, in a normal situation this would be an unlikely attack.

There are three basic punches you might encounter:

1. Jab
2. Hook
3. Uppercut

Then, if you were to look at the targets where you might expect to be attacked, there are really only two: the head and torso. I would venture a guess that most of the time the initial punch delivered in a self-defense situation is to the head. Could you reasonably expect a punch to the leg? I don't think so.

In general, it seems prudent to concentrate on practicing defensive tactics against techniques we can reasonably expect to occur.

I would like to reemphasize the point that you can logically expect to encounter only a relatively limited number of kinds of attacks. And I believe that the attacking techniques are predictable—they're probably the same today as they were a hundred years ago. We only have a limited number of ways in which we can try to do harm to another person. We have only two hands and two feet, and there are limits as to what we can do with them.

Making the Most of Your 20 Percent

As you become familiar with the 80/20 rule, you will begin to see many more instances where there are clear applications in your life. Time management may not be considered a natural subject for a book on the martial arts. However, how you manage your training time *is* relevant.

Simply put, martial arts training takes time. I would wager at some point in your life you have said something to the effect of, "I just wish there were more hours to the day." We all sometimes face the problem of fitting everything we want to accomplish into a short 24-hour day.

As an exercise, try to identify the things in your life that give you the most pleasure. You'll probably find that only a small part of your day is devoted to those moments. For example, most people work a five-day week—with only two days for rest and relaxation. Our work (or school) commitment lasts 7 or 8 hours per day. Factor in travel time of 30 minutes or more each way and you could spend 10 hours or more per day at work. Factor in the 6 to 8 hours of sleep you should be getting, and you end up with only 5 or 6 hours you can call your own.

And if you are responsible for taking care of others—if, for example, you are a parent—you will need to make sure the family's meals are prepared, groceries purchased, cleaning, maintenance, and other chores completed. By the time all of our time is accounted for we may end up with only a few hours to ourselves. The 80/20 ratio is starting to look more like 90/10!

Time, as you can see, is a precious commodity. It is therefore critical that you maximize the way you use your time. The amount of time you have to train, however, may not be as important as how you use that time.

For starters, you can analyze and adapt your training to fit your specific needs—so that you get more out of every session. Know your needs, and your interests, and try to make them the focus of your training program.

I would also like to offer you a simple tactic to make sure you get the most out of your development in the martial arts: We all have limits on the amount of time we can spend training. And we can expect to get a limited amount of time from any instructor. They face the same limits on their time—divided by the number of students they're trying to instruct. The primary responsibility for your development in the martial arts is, of course, yours. And your instructor inevitably plays a major role in your development. However, you also interact with many other individuals who can enhance your martial arts training—both in and out of your dojo. Use your time and relationships with other students and colleagues to see that you're all making the most of your precious time.

Develop relationships with peers whom you respect—you can share your training experiences with each other and help each other make the most of your training time. The following are some recommendations:

1. Find mentors who are willing to help you in areas where you do not have expertise. A good mentor would be an individual who is both senior to you in experience or training—and still willing to work with you! You can even benefit from working with a mentor who is junior to you, if that person has developed an area of expertise in which you are lacking. For example, if a member of your karate dojo is skilled in wrestling, you may want to have that person mentor you in the area of ground fighting.

2. Become a mentor for others in your group. Each of us has our own particular skill or area of expertise that would be useful to others. Know what your skills are, and you'll know how you can help others as a mentor. Teaching or mentoring others has its rewards for you as well—it almost inevitably leads to a clearer and more sophisticated understanding of the material you're teaching.

3. Look for other skills or experiences you have that you can share to the benefit of others. Perhaps you are a white belt, but have a career that provides knowledge that would be of use to more senior students. For example, a white belt who is also a police officer would be able to share real-life examples of the kinds of violent situations that people encounter. Lawyers could help instructors understand the legal ramifications of what they teach. Physicians or nurses can offer their knowledge in the field of medicine. If every person is willing to offer his or her unique skills and knowledge to others, the additive effect will provide great benefits for everyone.

In the end, you are responsible for making the most of your limited time—of getting the 80 percent effect for your 20 percent of time. You'll find that picking and choosing how you spend your time and whom you spend it with can be a very powerful tool in your development as a martial artist.

I hope the relevance of this discussion of the 80/20 rule is obvious. In the second part of this book, I've taken the list of common attacks from the beginning of this chapter, and tried to show how the down block movement can be applied. Rather than surveying all of the different martial arts techniques that can be applied to self-defense, the book describes possible responses to the range of attacks that you're most likely to encounter—with defenses against kicks, grabs, and punches—based on variations in one central approach—the down block.

Again, one small part of your martial arts repertoire can be employed in a large number of common self-defense situations. And if you fit your training to that understanding, you should feel like the precious time you have for training is being used more efficiently and effectively.

Taking the Initiative

In the last chapter, I established a core group of techniques you are likely to see if attacked. Though this kind of analysis—and planning—is necessary, there is more to self-defense than physical movements. It's just as important to be mentally prepared for the onset of an attack.

One important concept related to the mental side of the martial arts is that of *sen* 先, which is commonly translated from the Japanese as "initiative."

Words in any language have multiple meanings (remember our earlier look at the word "chair"?), which in turn may vary from age to age. The word "initiative," for example, has a number of definitions:

1. A beginning or introductory step
2. An opening move
3. First action
4. The first action or movement, often intended to solve a problem
5. The initial or leading action in a process

The concept of sen, or initiative, is a critical one throughout the martial arts. In Japanese martial arts, you'll find three distinct uses of the term. Each represents a subtly different concept, and each deserves a closer look.

Go no Sen 後の先

In simple terms, *go no sen* means that once your opponent attacks, you defend yourself against the attack. While this sounds simple, in reality, blocking a fast punch can be difficult, if not impossible. The closer you are to your opponent, the harder it is to react quickly enough to his aggressive actions. If your opponent can reach out and touch your body without moving his feet, or shifting his body weight, he will be able to initiate an attack that will be virtually impossible to defend against.

Consider that once your opponent initiates a movement you must first recognize that an attack is in progress—your mind must process this information, formulate a defensive tactic, and then perform the defensive move. The closer your opponent is, the less time you have to work through these three steps.

As a practical matter, if you are in a situation where you may be required to defend yourself, you should avoid letting people get too close. If you do, it is highly likely that you can be struck, even if you are a highly trained martial artist. Many people believe that whoever lands the first telling attack will be the ultimate victor. Only if the attack does not immediately render you incapable of response, will you be able to retaliate and successfully defend yourself.

In law enforcement training, many instructors advise that you should not allow anyone within six feet of your person. They reason that it is quite difficult to react to a spontaneous attack within this distance.

Another aspect of go no sen is the idea of allowing your opponent to fully commit to his aggressive action, and then taking advantage of his movement. For example, your opponent may grab part of your body with the intention of controlling your mobility, and perhaps delivering a punch, kick, joint manipulation, or throwing technique.

While it may seem counterintuitive, when your opponent reaches out and grabs you, he is also offering you a substantial number of defensive possibilities.

For example, when a person grabs your lapel with his left hand, he will only be able to attack with his right hand. He would have to let go of your lapel to use his left! From the defensive perspective, you still have both your right and left hands free for techniques.

Don't discount the ability of your attacker to use his feet for aggressive action or for defensive purposes. If he doesn't use his legs as weapons he has effectively cut his options for potential attacks in half. Even if your opponent does use both his arms and legs to attack, his grab has still reduced his effective weapons by one-fourth. And this still gives you, as the person in the defensive position, a tactical advantage.

Keep in mind that when your aggressor reaches out and grabs you he also exposes vulnerable points on his own body. As the defender, you will be able to keep your hands and arms close to your body while, at the same time, attacking the arm of your opponent. There's no rule that says you have to extend your hand to your attacker's torso in order to begin an effective counterattack!

Another advantage of keeping your hands and arms close to your own body, while your aggressor's arm or arms are extended, is that it increases your strength. Consider how easy it is to hold a ten-pound weight close to your chest, as opposed to holding it extended from your body. As the defender, with your arms held close to your body, you have a substantial mechanical advantage over an attacker with his arm extended. As you can see, despite the risks, there are significant tactical advantages inherent in go no sen.

Sen no Sen 先 の 先

Sen no sen is the second aspect of this concept that deserves strategic consideration. It describes a moment of confrontation in which two opponents face each other with every intention of physical aggression. One is the aggressor, and the other on the defensive—but both are ready and able to inflict injury on the other. As the aggressor makes the mental commitment to attack and starts his movement, the defender does the same—simultaneously.

Before starting a physical attack, your opponent may try to intimidate you with predictable physical postures. These first indications are usually easy to identify and are often accompanied by verbal "puffing." The verbal threats may be as far as it goes if you can reach some kind of settlement or accommodation that prevents further violence. However, without a settlement, the threats are likely to escalate into a physical confrontation.

Some postures that indicate action is imminent are:

- Flushed face
- Head and neck pulled back
- Teeth bared in a snarling attitude
- Shallow, rapid breathing
- An empty or glazed look to the eyes
- Aggressive verbal behavior, such as yelling, cursing, taunts, or belligerent words
- Excessive eye contact during the conversation
- Vacillation between cooperative and uncooperative attitude
- Physically violent acts toward inanimate objects near to hand
- Attempts to incite individuals nearby into physical altercation

Quick reaction time and skill in reading your opponent's body language are critical to sen no sen.

Sen Sen no Sen 先々の先

In cases identified with *sen sen no sen*, you are able to prepare for your opponent's attack by reading the subtle cues offered by his body position and demeanor.

If you're an experienced martial artist, you'll be able to recognize, by body posture, what portions of your opponent's body could be used for attack. For example, if your opponent has his right leg back with his body facing to his right, it will be harder for him to initiate an attack with his right hand than with his left. If he does attack with his right hand, his arm will have to travel a greater distance before it reaches your body. Since his arm has to travel farther, you'll have more time to react to the aggressive movement.

In such a situation, you should expect your opponent to initiate his attack with his left hand, because it is the closest part of his body to you. If you know the attack will most likely come from his left hand, you are in a better position to respond to his aggressive movement. This doesn't mean that your opponent will not attack with his right hand, or even attack with either foot.

With training you will be able to read the subtle shifts in your opponent's balance and posture, which will give you some indication of the direction and form of his attack—often even before he recognizes it. In this kind of confrontation, understanding the probable form of the attack gives you a definite advantage. You can alter your body position to both reduce your opponent's advantage and slightly increase your own advantage.

For example, if you are confronted by an opponent as described above, where your opponent has his left side forward, you can alter your position so that you present a smaller target. Turning your body at a 45-degree angle to your opponent, with your right foot forward, offers your opponent a smaller target. It also puts parts of your body out of the range of immediate attack.

Another aspect to the concept of sen sen no sen is the idea that your opponent is ready and willing to attack you. As the defender, you must be just as ready and willing to defend yourself against his aggressive behavior.

In this situation, there is usually a split second between the moment your opponent makes a mental commitment to attack and his first move. This gives you an opportunity to initiate a defensive move. Your attack must be made first, in that split second between your opponent's thought and his action. His commitment to the attack will prevent him from responding with a defense, which gives you an important advantage.

In a self-defense situation that involves an element of sen sen no sen, the immediacy of your defense could prove to be a problem for witnesses to the event. While a trained martial artist can recognize when an attack is about to be initiated, an individual who is not as "tuned in" may see your defensive move as an attack. An untrained observer may think that you started the exchange because your defensive movement "beat them to the punch."

In situations where you feel you are in imminent danger of being attacked, it would probably be prudent to avoid or escape from the confrontation if at all possible. However, there are times when this won't be possible, and you'll have to defend yourself—or someone else. In these situations, where there's no chance of escape and you're at risk of suffering serious bodily harm, you may have to respond with physical force—whether or not a casual observer understands or appreciates the sequence of events.

It seems reasonable that if you're in a situation where you fear for your life, you should be able to use deadly force to defend yourself. And if the potential danger you face is less than deadly, then your response should be less than deadly.

However, you are obligated to learn and be guided by the laws that apply in your area. Each government or jurisdiction has specific laws covering self-defense, and part of your training should involve developing a full understanding of the laws that apply in your area.

This is just one example of how a seemingly simple martial arts concept can contain many complexities and subtleties. This is why focusing your training—whether on the subset of attacks you're more likely to encounter, or on something as seemingly limited as the down block—makes sense. By paying close attention to the complexities and subtleties of these basic aspects of your martial arts training, you'll develop a deeper understanding of techniques that may sometimes seem rigid and routine—and a more sophisticated and flexible repertoire of martial arts skills.

Part Two
Down Blocks

Down Block

The basic down block is made up of several motions. Down blocks can be performed with either the right or left hand.

Figure 1: To perform a down block, move your right hand (as shown here) out in front of your body. At the same time, retract the opposite hand to the side of your head or neck.

Figure 2: Then make the down block motion by moving your left hand down to cove the lower section of your body. At the same time, pull your right hand back to your hip.

Figure 3: In some forms you may bring your blocking hand to your side as shown here.

Figure 4: In many forms you would follow the block with a punch from the hand that is on your waist. While this is a separate move there can be examples of how this movement could be used in ways other than a punch.

In the following examples the form of a down block may not be followed exactly. But the major motions of the movement will be seen in the photographs. Remember, the exact form of the down block can change style-to-style and instructor-to-instructor.

Down Block 31

# 4 DEFENSE AGAINST A KICK

The most common bunkai of the down block is a defense against a front kick. I have shown four examples of possible defensive techniques against a kick.

Throughout this book the central theme will be the application of the movement of the down block and the various ways this simple motion can be utilized in the various self-defense scenarios.

Technique 1

The most basic of applications for a down block is often described as a block to a front kick. This sequence shows the explanation most often given for a "down block." It is a low-level explanation, and even a cursory examination of the technique will demonstrate serious flaws.

Figure 1-1: Here your opponent is facing you in a free-sparring stance, with a considerable distance between the two of you.

Figure 1-2: You observe your opponent preparing to deliver a front kick. You pull your left hand back toward your right ear, and your right hand moves forward.

Figure 1-3: As your opponent fully extends his left leg you block the kick with your left hand.

This application can work, but it does leave you with the question "Is this the primary application for a down block?" In my opinion, while this technique could work, it is not the primary bunkai I would make use of in my study of kata.

Anyone who has done any sparring will be able to recognize the major fault in this technique. You will not have time to "chamber" your left hand all the way back to your right ear and then block your opponent's kick. If you truly believe you can do this, simply ask a training partner to perform a front kick. You will find that it is very difficult to perform all of the motions and still block the kick. So, from my perspective, this is a low-level explanation and should not be given serious consideration.

If we accept that this is a technique of little value, then it would seem logical that there must be more effective bunkai we can explore. I want to keep in mind that in cases where the attack may not be a kick, but rather some other form of attack, this basic movement of the down block may provide alternate solutions to various attacks.

Technique 2

The basic movement of a down block can be used against a front kick with some minor modifications. The initial movement (the chambering action) can be used to strike the inside of your opponent's ankle. The typical blocking portion of the movement could then be used in two different ways. Your elbow could strike the leg, and then you could strike the leg with a hammer fist.

Figure 2–1: You are facing your opponent at a medium distance.

Figure 2–2: Your opponent kicks at your chest with the right foot. Shift your weight to the rear and deflect the kick with your left hand.

Figure 2–3: Punch to Spleen 6 (**Figure 2a**) with your right fist. This should cause your opponent enough pain to make him to lose his balance.

Figure 2–4: Continue the motion of your right hand so your arm crosses over the opponent's leg. Once your arm is past the leg strike back on the leg with your elbow.

Figure 2-5: Continue the motion of your elbow strike so your fist strikes the back of the opponent's upper thigh and forces him toward the ground.

Figure 2-6: If you maintain your grip on the opponent's leg, you will be able to continue on with another technique if it is needed.

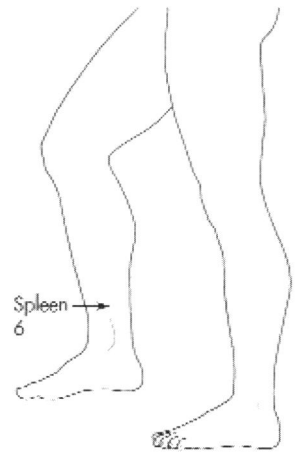

Technique 3

It is important to realize that the action of your hand moving back toward your head in the typical chamber motion can be used in ways other than to "generate power." By thinking outside of the box, you will be able to find options for defensive movements that might otherwise not be apparent. This is the objective of this book, to give alternative examples of how the same movement of the down block can be used in various defensive techniques. You will see how the basic movement stays the same, and you will be able to defend yourself against a variety of attacks.

Defense Against a Kick

Figure 3–1: Your opponent prepares to attack you with a side kick.

Figure 3–2: The kick is delivered to your solar plexus. Draw your right hand up and under the opponent's leg to strike Spleen 6 (see Figure 2a) with your right fist. At the same time strike down with your left hand and grab the opponent's ankle.

Figure 3–3: Continue the motion of your right hand, and bring your right fist up toward your left side.

Figure 3–4: Strike down on your opponent's upper thigh at the tip of Gall Bladder 31 (**Figure 3a**) to collapse your opponent's leg.

Figure 3–5: You could follow through with a hammer fist strike to the groin.

38 75 Down Blocks

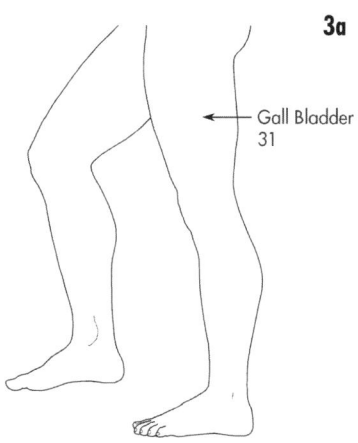

Gall Bladder 31

Technique 4

The following technique makes use of body motion to help you avoid the initial attack of your opponent. By turning your body to the side, you help remove the target presented to your opponent.

Figure 4–1: Your opponent prepares to deliver a front kick with his right foot.

Figure 4–2: As your opponent chambers his foot, turn your body to the side and sidestep toward your left.

Figure 4–3: Deflect your opponent's right hand with the chambering action of your left hand. At the same time scoop his ankle with your right hand, pulling your hand toward your hip.

Figure 4–4: By maintaining control of your opponent's right leg, you should be able to disrupt his balance as you step forward.

Figure 4–5: Continue to sweep your left hand downward, as in a down block motion, to throw your opponent.

40 75 Down Blocks

Defense Against a Same-Side Wrist Grab

One of the most common ways an individual will attempt to control your movement is to grab your wrist, arm, or lapel. The following seven techniques will illustrate a number of responses to an opponent's grabbing you in a "same-side" wrist grab. A same-side grab occurs when your opponent grabs your right side with his left hand, or when your left side is grabbed with the opponent's right hand. In other words the opponent's arm does not cross your body.

Technique 5

Many times, a direct action can work very well in a self-defense situation. This technique is quite simple and, at the same time, very effective.

Figure 5–1: Your opponent grabs your right wrist with his left hand.

Figure 5–2: Chamber your right hand, which should begin to loosen your opponent's grip or even completely dislodge it.

Figure 5–3: Using your left forearm, strike your opponent's left forearm, or you could target Large Intestine 11 (**Figure 5a**). This should dislodge his grip and begin to turn his body in a clockwise direction.

Figure 5–4: You can maintain contact with his left forearm with your forearm or grab his sleeve. At the same time, execute a punch to a target of opportunity, such as Stomach 9 (**Figure 5b**). Or, if you can, strike any of the soft tissue areas of the neck. If possible, strike soft tissue with your fist. Conversely, if you must strike a bony area of your opponent's body, use a portion of your body that is padded with muscle or a heavy layer of tissue to lessen the chance of injury to yourself.

DEFENSE AGAINST A SAME-SIDE WRIST GRAB   43

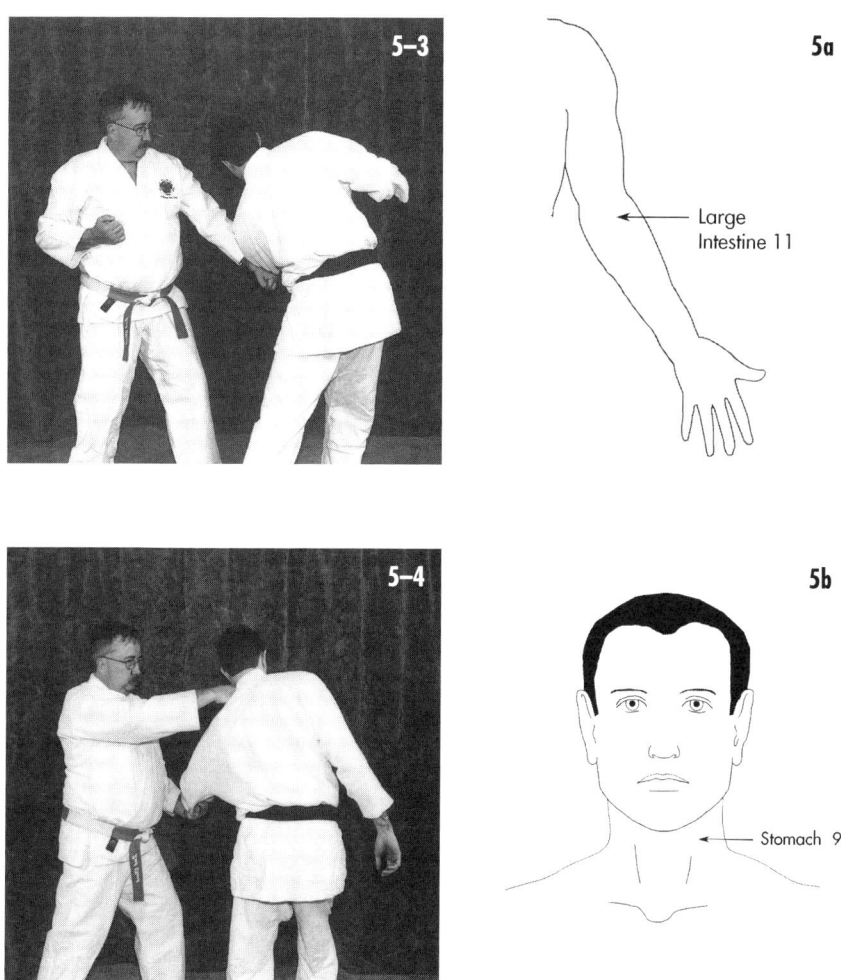

TECHNIQUE 6

Many times in self-defense situations you will find that a portion of your body is grabbed while your opponent threatens you with his other hand. In such situations, remember that once your opponent has grabbed a portion of your body, he cannot use that hand to strike you. Also, there is an advantage to you in that you can respond more quickly to tactile stimulation than to visual stimulation. A well-trained judoka can read an opponent's body position and react very quickly to the opponent's action. It is not a disadvantage if your opponent grabs your wrist; in fact, with many techniques, it is imperative that the opponent does grab a portion of your body. Consider the fact that you can grab your opponent's arm much more easily when he has a firm hold on some portion of your clothing or anatomy—it is much harder to grab a moving arm or leg.

Figure 6–1: Your opponent grabs your left wrist with his right hand and prepares to strike you with his left hand.

Figure 6–2: Rotate your left hand over the top of your opponent's right hand so you are gabbing his wrist with your left hand. If you are trained in pressure points, you can apply pressure to the points located on the wrist with the side of your thumb or with the base of your index finger. The point you would be attacking is Lung 7 (**Figure 6a**).

Figure 6–3: Once your opponent begins to bend down from the pressure applied to the wrist points, bring your right arm toward your left side.

Figure 6–4: This will allow you to strike the outside portion of your opponent's arm, just above the elbow.

Defense Against a Same-Side Wrist Grab   45

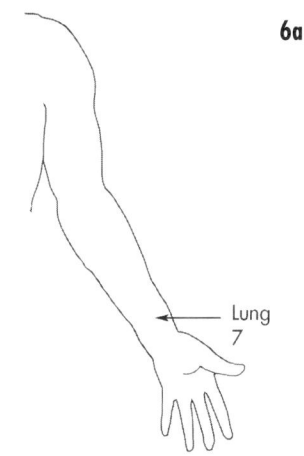

Technique 7

Once again, if you are in a situation where your wrist is grabbed, you can use it to your advantage. If your opponent is determined to hold onto your wrist, it is possible to pull him off-balance and disrupt his attempt to strike you with his other hand.

Figure 7–1: Your opponent has grabbed your left wrist and is preparing to strike you in the face with his left hand.

Figure 7–2: Roll your left hand over the top of your opponent's right hand and grab your opponent's right wrist again.

Figure 7–3: Quickly bring your right fist up toward your opponent's head and strike the side of his neck or face with your right fist.

Figure 7–4: As you pull your right fist back toward your left side, drop the tip of your right elbow onto your opponent's solar plexus.

Figure 7–5: As your opponent bends over from the strike to the solar plexus, strike the side of his neck with your right forearm.

Figure 7–6: This view shows you how you can grip your opponent's opposite hand. By pressing with the base of your hand on the little-finger side of your opponent's hand, you can cause him a great deal of pain.

DEFENSE AGAINST A SAME-SIDE WRIST GRAB   47

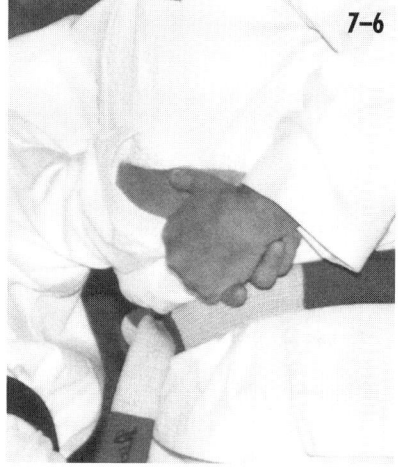

Technique 8

This defense has you circling your arm out of a wrist grab. This is a great example of a situation in which you should use your whole body instead of just the strength of your arm. Being able to move your arm in such a manner also allows you to make use of your elbow. That is to say, push your elbow and let your hand follow the action of your arm. The harder your opponent attempts to hold onto your wrist, the better this technique will work. When the opponent holds your wrist very tightly, it allows you to apply a one-handed wrist lock.

Figure 8–1: Your opponent has grabbed your right hand with his left hand.

Figure 8–2: Circle your right hand to the outside of his wrist. When you do this, be sure not to use only the strength of your arm, but rather make use of body shifting to allow you to use the muscles of your body and, equally important, your body weight.

Figure 8–3: Once you are able to apply pressure on your opponent's wrist, his natural reaction is to move in a way that relieves the pressure on the wrist. You need only cause momentary pain to the wrist to get him to bend forward slightly. Then, by placing your hand on top of his head, you can direct his movement in the direction you wish.

Figure 8–4: Your left hand begins to come back toward your waist as it pushes your opponent's head down and in front of your body.

Figure 8–5: By moving your right hand forward and pulling your left hand back, you will cause your opponent to lose his balance and fall. This fall could be directed at several angles.

Defense Against a Same-Side Wrist Grab   49

Technique 9

Once again, this technique will rely on your opponent's holding onto your wrist with a determined grip. However, by grabbing onto the opponent's sleeve, you will be able to obtain more control over your opponent.

Figure 9–1: Your opponent has grabbed your right wrist with his left hand.

Figure 9–2: Grab onto his sleeve with your left hand as you pull it back toward your waist. Your right hand will pull back in a chambering motion; be careful to allow your opponent to maintain contact with your wrist.

Figure 9–3: Continue to pull back with your left hand, and apply pressure to your opponent's wrist. This is accomplished by making sure that his wrist is bent and his thumb is pressed in and toward the center of his body.

Figure 9–3a: This is a close-up view of the hand position.

Figure 9–4: By pressing down on your opponent's thumb with your right forearm, you will be able to cause enough pain to throw your opponent toward his rear section.

Defense Against a Same-Side Wrist Grab 51

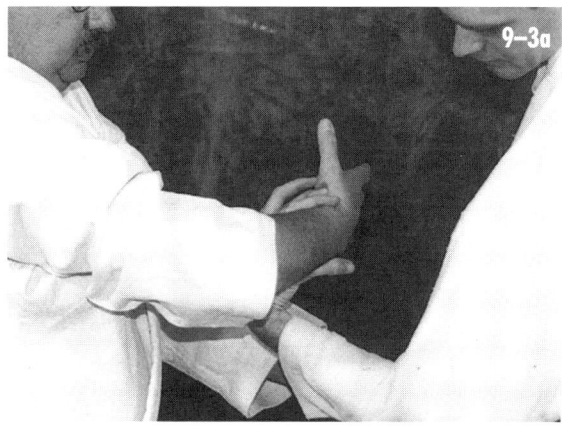

Technique 10

This technique, like many, will rely on your opponent's intention to forcefully grab and maintain his grip on your wrist. Remember, in practice, you will rely on your partner to simulate a strong and determined grip. Another point to remember is that, when someone grabs your arm, he intends to control your movement either by restraining further movement or by moving you into a position of his choice.

Figure 10–1: Your opponent grabs your right hand with his left and prepares to strike you with his right hand.

Figure 10–2: Allow your opponent to maintain his grip, and at the same time pivot your body toward his left side. Try to keep your hand in the same area; do not pull or push your hand into a different plane. However, as you turn, allow your forearm to begin to apply pressure on the little-finger side of your opponent's hand. Once your elbow passes over the top of your opponent's forearm begin to apply pressure toward the ground.

Figures 10–2a, 10–2b, 10–2c, and 10–2d: Note how the position of the lock is similar to nikyo. Nikyo (sometimes Kikajo) is the Japanese term for one of five basic immobilization techniques used in aikido. Nikyo refers to the second of these techniques—the position of your opponent's wrist and arm forms an "S" shape, and pressure is applied to the wrist. You will want to turn your opponent's wrist toward his head, and at the same time press down on your opponent's forearm, as seen in Figure 10–2b. To increase the pressure on your opponent's wrist, you can increase the pain by applying force in a circular direction. In Figures 10–2c and 10–2d, you will notice the forefinger is extended. This is done only for the example, in order to demonstrate the direction of pressure to be brought against your opponent's wrist. In reality you would keep your fingers near your opponent's wrist, as in Figure 10–2b.

Figure 10–3: As your opponent begins to become conscious of the pain from the grip, one of two things will occur: (1) he will release his grip or (2) he will attempt to maintain his grip. The latter will allow this technique to proceed. Notice the opponent's knees will begin to bend if the grip is maintained.

Defense Against a Same-Side Wrist Grab 53

Figure 10-3a: Note how pressure can be applied to your opponent's forearm, even if his grip has started to open.

Figure 10-4: Step to the left-rear side of your opponent and continue to put pressure on his wrist. By bringing your right hand down toward his face, you will cause him to lose his balance toward his left rear. Continued motion will cause him to lose his balance completely and fall to the ground.

54 75 Down Blocks

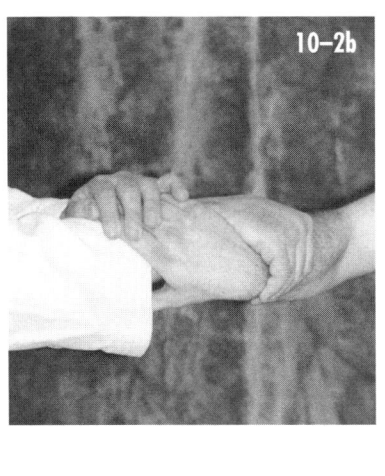
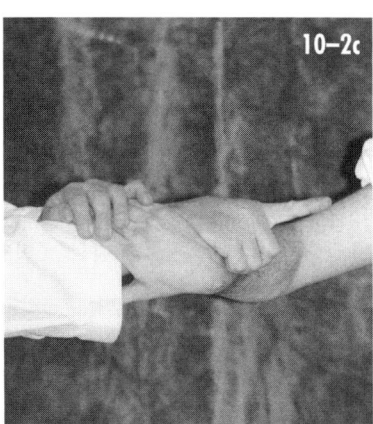
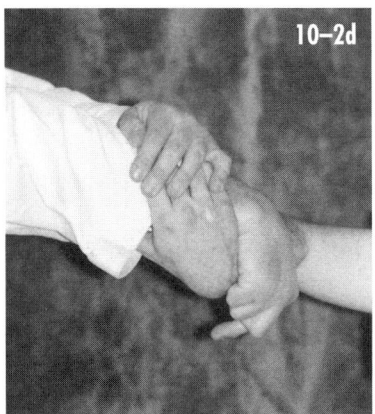

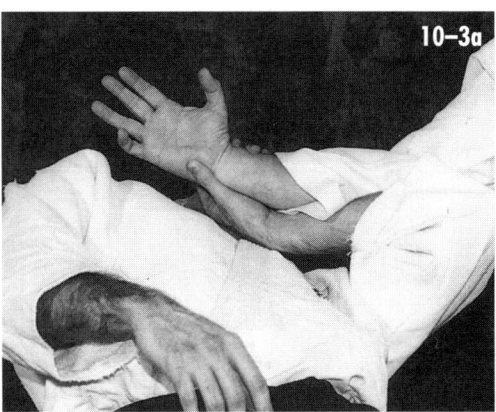

Defense Against a Same-Side Wrist Grab   55

Technique 11

In self-defense, there may be times when your opponent will threaten you by bringing his hands up in a threatening position. This may be in preparation to an actual attack, or it may be nothing more than a posture your opponent assumes to intimidate you into submission.

Figure 11–1: Your opponent brings his hands up in a threatening manner. Respond by raising your hands in a defensive position in front of your face.

Figure 11–2: There are times when you can offer an opportunity for your opponent to attack you in such a way as to give yourself an advantage. In this scenario, you rely on the natural reaction of your opponent to grab your arm when it is placed within a few inches of his hand. You are looking for your opponent to grab your forward (right) hand.

Figure 11–3: Immediately grab his left wrist with your left hand, and press your elbow forward toward his face. This will allow you to put pressure on his wrist.

Figure 11–4: Continue to pull back with your left hand, and increase the pressure on his wrist. Notice that, with this lock, you will apply pressure on the area of the little finger with the back of your forearm.

Figure 11–5: As your opponent goes to the ground, you can pull back on his left hand, which will contribute to his loss of balance. At the same time, use a hammer fist to the side of the neck (Stomach 9 (see Figure 5b)) or to the jaw (Stomach 5 (**Figure 11a**)). Of course, if other targets of opportunity present themselves for a strike, do not hesitate to conform to the situation.

56   75 Down Blocks

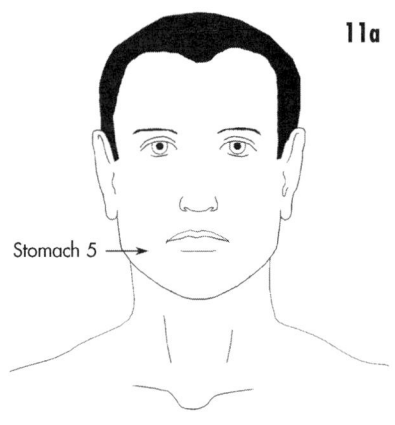

Stomach 5

6 DEFENSE AGAINST A CROSS-HAND WRIST GRAB

As in the previous section, we will look at seven different responses that could be utilized against a cross-hand grab to the wrist. "Cross-hand" refers to any grab that has your opponent grabbing your right wrist with his right hand, or your left wrist with his left hand. Cross-hand grabs would seem to be less likely to occur than same-side grabs, because cross-hand grabs require your opponent to reach across your body, which could make it more difficult to attack you with the opposite hand. There may be situations in which you can present yourself in such a way as to offer your opponent this type of grab for a tactical advantage on your part.

Technique 12

Many times a very simple technique is more than adequate to stop a confrontation or to place yourself in a better position to defend yourself. This technique does not require a great deal of skill to apply, but it is not a technique that would offer you a way to persuade your opponent to desist his aggression. However, it does offer you a technique that could be valuable in a situation where a great deal of force is not justified.

Figure 12–1: Your opponent has grabbed your right wrist with his left hand.

Figure 12–2: Pull your right hand back to your waist, and at the same time bring your left hand into a position to strike your opponent's forearm.

Figure 12–3: You can strike any point on the wrist (Lung 7 (see Figure 6a)), forearm (Lung 5 (**Figure 12a**)), or upper arm (Lung 3 (**Figure 12b**)). Mainly, the choice of target would reflect the distance between you and your opponent.

Defense Against a Cross-Hand Wrist Grab   59

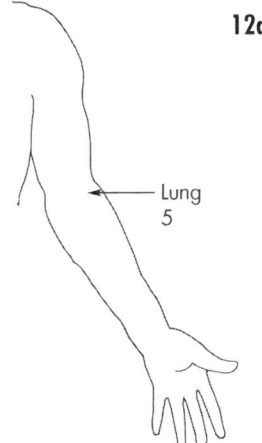

12a

Lung 5

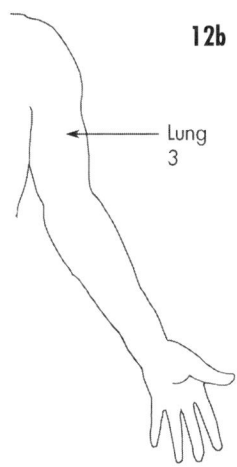

12b

Lung 3

Technique 13

In a situation where your opponent has you in a cross-hand grab, he has placed himself at a slight disadvantage. If your opponent is going to throw a hook punch toward your face, his punch will have to cross his center line to make contact with your head. By moving your body toward your right side, you will increase the distance his punch must travel to make contact with your head. As a consequence, it will give you more time to react to his aggressive actions, it can reduce the amount of power he can generate, and he will be in a more unbalanced position.

Figure 13-1: From a cross-hand wrist grab, your opponent may try to pull you forward and punch you in the face.

Figure 13-2: If your opponent has you by the left wrist, step forward with your right leg. At the same time, bring your right arm up and under his left elbow. As you do this grab his wrist again with your left hand, and pull it toward your waist.

Figure 13-3: Strike down with a hammer fist to his groin or other point of his body.

Defense Against a Cross-Hand Wrist Grab

13-2

13-3

Technique 14

This technique is an example of how the typical down block can be used along with the reverse punch in self-defense.

Figure 14–1: Your opponent has grabbed your right wrist in a cross-hand grab and is threatening to punch you in the face.

Figure 14–2: Rotate your right hand up and toward your forehead, as in a chamber motion.

Figure 14–3: Bring your right hand down toward your right leg as you roll your opponent's hand over and down toward your leg.

Figure 14–4: As you pull your hand back toward your waist, you can punch to your opponent's side in the floating rib area.

Technique 15

Figure 15-1: Your opponent has grabbed your left wrist in a cross-hand grab.

Figure 15-2: Rotate your left arm in a counterclockwise direction. At the same time, begin to step forward at a 45-degree angle with your right foot and bring your right arm up toward your head. With this motion, you could strike your opponent's upper arm with your right forearm to cause him to lose his concentration and to begin to turn him toward his right side.

Figure 15-3: Grab his left wrist with your left hand. As you bring your arm down, you could strike the upper portion of his arm with the tip of your elbow to begin to force his arm down.

Figure 15-4: As your right foot continues to come forward, continue applying pressure just above his elbow (golgi tendon) with your right forearm.

Technique 16

Figure 16-1: Your opponent has grabbed your right wrist and threatens you with his left hand. Since your opponent will not be able to strike you with the hand he has grabbed you with, you will want to avoid the hand that could possibly strike you.

Figure 16-2: To increase the distance between your opponent's hand and your body, step forward. At the same time, roll your right hand over the top of

Defense Against a Cross-Hand Wrist Grab

your opponent's grip, pushing against his thumb. This should enable you to release his grip on your wrist. As you bring your left arm up in the chamber position, you can strike his upper arm with your elbow.

Figure 16–3: Strike down over your opponent's neck area with your left forearm. As you step forward, make contact with his body to upset his balance.

Figure 16–4: Grab his right arm or sleeve with your right hand and pull his arm back; continue the downward motion of your left arm to throw him to the ground.

Technique 17

Figure 17-1: In this situation, your right wrist is grabbed by your opponent's right hand.

Figure 17-2: Bring your right hand up toward your face in a circular motion. Bring your left hand up to grip your opponent's hand as it comes free.

Figure 17-3: Your left hand will grab your opponent's hand to apply sankyo, and your right wrist will begin to press down on his arm. Sankyo is the third of the basic or foundation techniques of aikido. It is applied by grabbing your opponent's hand, as illustrated in Figure 17-3, and twisting the little-finger side of the hand back toward his body. To apply pressure in the most effective way, you will want to keep your opponent's elbow higher than his shoulder. It is also important not to allow his arm to form less than a 90-degree angle. If you do, this reduces the pressure on your opponent, so he could counter your defensive tactic. You will also find a discussion of this immobilization in Technique 60.

Figure 17-3a: This is a close-up view of how you can use your thumb to press on Large Intestine 4 (**Figure 17a**) to produce extra pain for sankyo.

Figure 17-4: Use your right forearm to press your opponent to the ground and maintain the lock on your opponent's hand.

DEFENSE AGAINST A CROSS-HAND WRIST GRAB

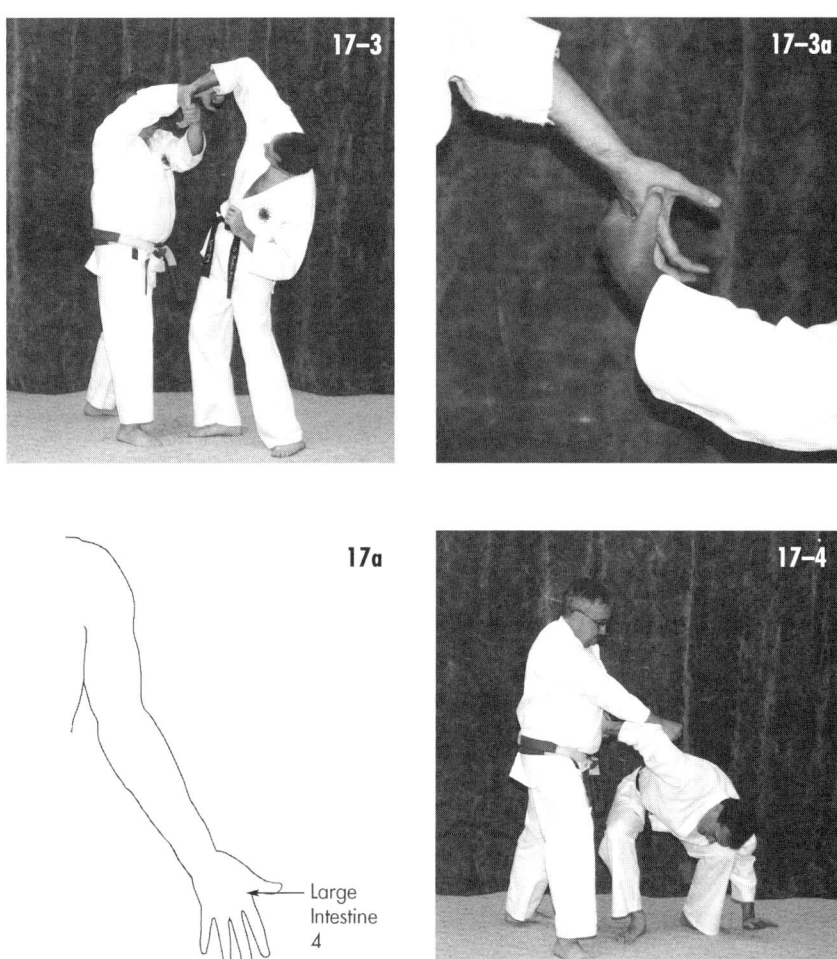

TECHNIQUE 18

This technique is a classic example of how cross-training can be extremely useful for any martial artist. Several of my students attended a seminar presented by J. K. Yamaue Soke of Yamaue-ryu Aiki Jutsu. As they demonstrated the technique, I noticed how the movement of the hand followed the form of a down block. At a later date, I was able to observe the same technique being taught by Jun Takami, Shihan of Hakko-Ryu. While I do not practice either of these two systems, it was possible to link the techniques from the two different systems to the down block.

It is important to note that the technique looks as if you require a compliant partner; however, if performed correctly, the thumb is locked into a position that will apply a great deal of pain to your opponent and allow you to take him to the ground. This same technique can be applied to a two-handed grab (see Technique 20).

Figure 18–1: In this position your opponent has grabbed your right wrist with his right hand.

Figure 18–2: Roll your forearm in such a way as to point your palm toward your face. This will help to bend your opponent's wrist, which is critical to the technique. As you bring your right hand back toward your face, visualize your hand making a movement in the air that resembles a "Z" or a question mark. Once your opponent's wrist is bending, begin to apply pressure on his thumb.

Figure 18–2a: This is a closeup of the movement in Figure 18–2.

Figure 18–3: Continue to apply pressure with your right hand, and force him toward the ground.

Figure 18–4: As your arm fully extends, your opponent should be on his knees or thrown toward the ground.

Defense Against a Cross-Hand Wrist Grab

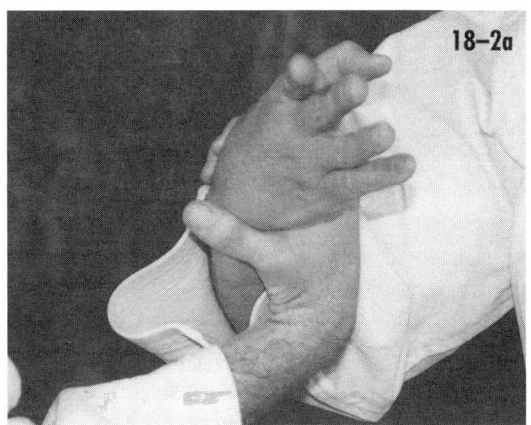

Defense Against a Double-Wrist Grab

This section will cover seven different examples of how you could be attacked with a double-hand grab. Once again, the techniques will mimic the movement of a normal "down block." Remember, a down block can be performed in a number of different ways depending on the style or system of martial arts you practice. These techniques are meant to stimulate your thought process so you can begin to develop techniques appropriate to your style and particular needs.

Technique 19

In this technique, there is a bit more body movement than in some of the others. However, this amount of body movement is not rare, and in the various kata you will find many examples of turns in conjunction with a down block.

Figure 19–1: Your opponent grabs your right hand with both hands.

Figure 19–2: Keep your right hand in virtually the same place and, at the same time, pivot on your right foot in a counterclockwise manner so that you and your opponent are facing the same direction. Your right hand will move forward slightly as you do this motion. It should cause your opponent to loosen his grip on your arm and move forward a bit.

Figure 19–3: Turn clockwise to face your opponent. Pivot on your left foot and step to your opponent's side with your right foot. As your opponent's grip is broken, grab his wrist with your right hand.

Figure 19–4: Continue your movement and grip your opponent's sleeve just above the elbow.

Figure 19–5: Press down with your left hand and pull back with your right to force your opponent to the ground.

Technique 20

This technique is virtually the same as Technique 18. As with many techniques, it is possible to make use of the same movement in various situations. For example, as you practice this technique, you can have a stick or knife in your

Defense Against a Double-Wrist Grab   73

hand and have your opponent attempt to stop you from stabbing or striking; as he grabs your wrist you will be able to counter his technique and continue on with your attack.

You may notice that it is less difficult to perform this technique than a single-hand grab. As you execute this technique, your opponent's hands begin to overlap and one of his hands applies pressure to the other hand.

Figure 20–1: Your opponent grabs your right hand with both of his hands.

Figure 20–2: Push your elbow forward and rotate your hand so that your palm is toward your face. Lock your opponent's thumb.

Figure 20–3: Continue the downward motion of your hand to take him to the ground.

Technique 21

As in previous examples, your opponent is attempting to control your movement by grabbing both of your wrists. As with all techniques that attempt to control your opponent, this technique will work best if your opponent is truly trying to grab your wrist and maintain control. If he does not intend to maintain his grip, this technique will simply release your wrist from his grip.

Figure 21–1: Your opponent grabs both of your wrists.

Figure 21–2: Begin to pull your left hand back toward your waist. At the same time rotate your right hand up and over your opponent's wrist.

Figure 21–3: If he is grabbing your wrist with intensity and maintains his grip, you can begin to apply a wrist lock (*nikyo*). (For a closer look at a lock performed in a similar manner, please refer to Figure 10–2a.)

Figure 21–4: As he bends, direct his balance toward his left-rear quadrant. If you can get his weight placed on his left foot and his knees bent, you will be able to push him to the ground.

TECHNIQUE 22

As in the previous example, your opponent has grabbed both of your wrists in an effort to control your body movement.

Figure 22-1: Your opponent grabs both of your wrists.

Figure 22-2: Move your left hand in a counterclockwise manner, and grab your opponent's wrist; begin to draw your left hand back toward your left side. In a coordinated movement, roll your right hand over the top of your opponent's wrist.

Figure 22-3: Pull your left hand back toward your left side. At the same time, roll your opponent's arm down and toward your knee.

Figure 22-4: At this point in the technique, you will need to feel for the position of your opponent's right arm. There will be a spot where, if you push forward with your left hand, you will feel the arm lock into the shoulder. When you are able to find this point, you will be able to push your opponent's balance over his left, front foot. Then, by pulling back slightly with your right hand, you will cause your opponent to lose his balance.

Figure 22-5: Once he has been thrown to the ground, you can chose to follow with a lock or another technique.

Technique 23

Figure 23–1: In this instance, your opponent grabs both of your wrists. There is no substantial difference between this and a single-hand grab to your wrist.

Figure 23–2: Grip your opponent's left wrist with your right hand; you need not disengage your opponent's grip on your right hand. It will not be difficult for a weaker individual to move his left hand to secure this grip, and your opponent will find it difficult to resist movement in this direction. There is an added advantage to allowing your opponent to maintain his grip on your wrist: he will not be able to punch you with that hand!

Figure 23–3: As you apply pressure to his little finger with the back of your forearm, you may notice an opportunity to strike targets, such as the side of the face, with your elbow. Do not hesitate to make use of such a strike in a self-defense situation.

Figure 23–3a: In this close-up of Figure 23–3, note how you can twist your opponent's wrist in a clockwise manner with your left hand and, at the same time, apply pressure in a counterclockwise manner to the little-finger portion of his hand with your right forearm. This provides an extremely effective way of applying pressure to your opponent.

Figure 23–4: Once your opponent has dropped to his knees, it is possible to strike the side of his neck or head with your hammer fist.

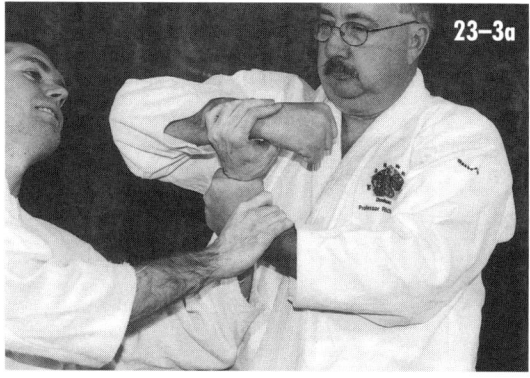

Technique 24

If you have both of your hands up to protect your face, many times your opponent will grab one or both of your wrists to attempt to control your movement. Also, he may try to push you backward off-balance. If you know this is a typical response of an opponent, you can use this to your advantage.

Figure 24-1: Your opponent has grabbed both of your wrists, and your hands are up to protect your face.

Figure 24-2: As is characteristic of this type of grip, your opponent will have his thumbs together. By turning your body in a clockwise fashion, begin to place your body at a 45-degree angle to your opponent. This will keep you from facing his force head on. Grab his right hand with your right hand—your thumb should be between his thumb and forefinger. Once you have established your grip, you can chamber your left hand toward your right ear. This will allow you to apply pressure on his wrist with your forearm.

Figure 24-3: Once his grip has been broken, you can release your left wrist and rotate his right hand to the right side of your body.

Figure 24-4: You can then strike the side of his neck or head, or the back of his neck, with a hammer fist strike of your left hand.

Technique 25

In the event that your opponent grabs both your wrist and upper arm, this technique provides you with an opportunity to use your arm in a unique manner. For this technique, you will use your right arm to apply force in two different directions at the same time. Your upper arm will push your opponent's left hand back, and at the same time, you will pull your opponent's right hand forward. This type of movement can cause your opponent to lose his balance with considerable ease.

Figure 25–1: Your opponent has grabbed your arm in an attempt to control your movement.

Figure 25–2: Rotate your body toward the rear, putting your weight on your left leg. At the same time, push your right elbow forward and rotate your palm back toward your face. This will allow you to swing your right hand back toward your head in a motion similar to the chamber of the down block.

Figure 25–3: Keeping your right hand high, begin to rotate your palm toward your opponent's face. It is possible to strike your opponent's solar plexus area at this time. Grab your opponent's wrist with your right hand, and twist his wrist in the direction of the little finger.

Figure 25–3a: This is a close-up of the movement in Figure 25–3.

Figure 25–4: Step forward with your right foot and begin to sweep your right arm down in a down block motion to throw.

DEFENSE AGAINST AN UPPER-ARM GRAB

In the following five examples, your opponent will be grabbing your upper arm. This type of attack can be seen as a preliminary movement, to be followed by a punch to the face or body. When defending against such attacks, you should not become so preoccupied with the grab that you disregard the possibility of a punch.

Technique 26

This is a typical example of how your opponent might grab your upper arm. When your opponent grabs you, he will most likely pull or push your arm in some fashion; you need to be prepared for this action.

Figure 26–1: Your opponent has grabbed the upper part of your left arm.

Figure 26–2: Bring your left hand up so that you lock your opponent's right hand to your chest. At the same time punch Heart 2 (**Figure 26a**) with your right fist.

Figure 26–3: Allow your fist to pass over the top of your opponent's right arm.

Figure 26–4: Strike Triple Warmer 13 (**Figure 26b**) with the tip of your elbow.

Figure 26–5: Strike Spleen 21 (**Figure 26c**) or another target of opportunity with your right hammer fist.

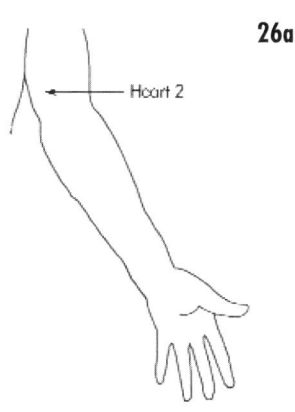

26a

84 75 Down Blocks

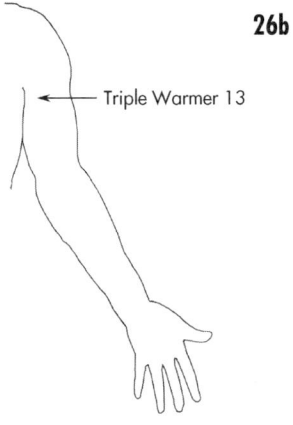

Triple Warmer 13

26b

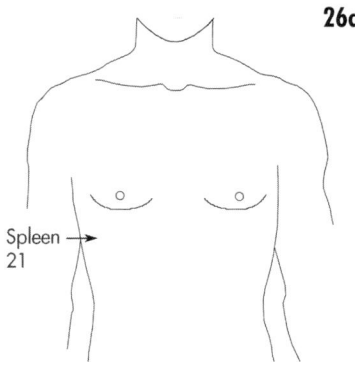

Spleen 21

26c

Technique 27

In this example, your opponent's arm is more extended when he grabs your upper arm. One thing to consider when your opponent's arm is extended is the possibility of causing him to lose his balance by shifting your weight so as to pull his weight over his forward toe. If your opponent's arm is bent, such a technique is not possible.

Figure 27-1: Your opponent grabs your left upper arm with his right hand.

Figure 27-2: Reach over and grab the top of your opponent's hand so that your thumb is between his thumb and forefinger. At the same time, press his hand onto your left arm so that he is unable to remove his hand.

Figure 27-3: Move your left foot forward toward your opponent. At the same time, place your left hand above his arm, and maintain your grip on his right hand.

Figure 27-4: By pressing your left hand down and twisting your right hand in a clockwise manner, you will effectively lock your opponent's wrist and force him to the ground.

Figure 27-4a: This is a reverse view so you can clearly see the technique. Notice that your left hand is in close proximity to your opponent's head and neck, which would allow you to strike these points as you execute the technique.

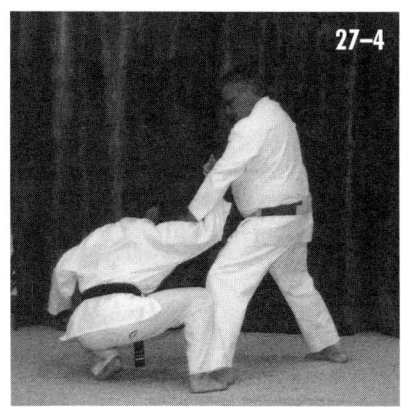

Technique 28

Once again your opponent has grabbed you with his arm approaching full extension.

Figure 28–1: Your opponent grabs your upper arm with his left hand.

Figure 28–2: Apply pressure with a rub to a point just above the elbow and to the side of your opponent's arm with your knuckles. This should cause your opponent's arm to bend. One point to remember with this technique is to push your opponent's left hand forward with your upper arm. This creates pressure against his hand, allowing this technique to be performed.

Defense Against an Upper-Arm Grab

Figure 28–3: Roll your right arm over the top of his elbow and apply pressure downward. Use your left hand to push his head in front of your stomach.

Figure 28–4: Slide your left arm on top of his left arm and continue to turn your opponent.

Figure 28–5: Allow your arm to slide back to his wrist. If you have your opponent's palm facing away from your body, you can pull back on his arm, which will apply pressure against the joint.

Figure 28–6: Deliver a hammer fist strike to the neck or side of the face with your right hand.

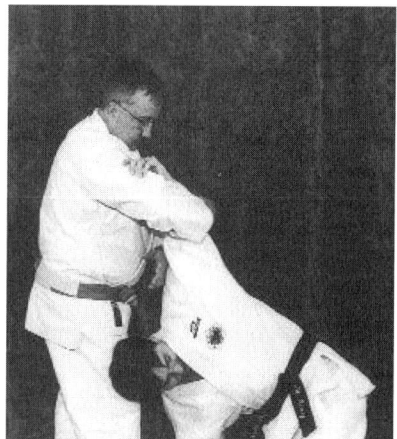

Technique 29

In this sequence, there are two examples of using a down block motion.

Figure 29–1: Your opponent has grabbed your arm at the elbow.

Figure 29–2: Similarly to the movement in Technique 24, circle your right hand up and over the top of your opponent's arm.

Figure 29–3: As you bring your arm down, lock your opponent's arm in a hammerlock.

Figure 29–3a: This shows the technique from the opposite view.

Figure 29–4: If you do not apply sufficient force when using this technique, your opponent may be able to turn his body in such a way as to attempt to strike you with his elbow or fist.

Figure 29–5: Deflect the oncoming attack with your left forearm and maintain the lock on his arm with your right hand. Allow your arm to slide along his arm to the point where you can grab his wrist with your left hand.

Figure 29–6: Once his wrist is grabbed with your left hand, pull his arm back in a direction that is forward of your body causing your opponent's arm to lock.

Figure 29–7: Allow your opponent to spin out of the hammerlock. Maintain control of his left wrist with your right hand, and apply an arm bar by pressing down on his elbow with your left hand.

Defense Against an Upper-Arm Grab

Technique 30

Unlike in the previous examples of an upper-arm grab, your opponent is now to your side and facing the same direction. You might find yourself in a situation like this if a person is trying to escort you out of a location. However, this is a dangerous position for him because he does not have you in some type of pain compliance technique.

Figure 30-1: Your opponent is facing the same direction as you and grabs your left upper arm with his right hand.

Figure 30-2: Turn toward your opponent and, at the same time, raise your left hand up and toward the right side of your head. Your right hand will come up and under your left arm to grab your opponent's hand. Your thumb should be at his wrist, and your fingers should grip the thumb portion of his hand.

Figure 30-3: Twist his wrist to bend him toward his right side.

Figure 30-4: Strike down on his neck with your elbow as you step forward. Continue the motion of your hand to throw him to the ground.

Defense Against an Upper-Arm Grab 91

9 PREEMPTIVE TECHNIQUES

The scenarios presented in the following pages give examples of sen sen no sen as described in Chapter 3. I would like to take this opportunity to remind you how vitally important it is to be familiar with the laws pertaining to self-defense. I do not claim to be a lawyer nor do I give legal advice on what you should do in any situation where you feel you must defend yourself. I have determined in what situations I would defend others or myself and to what length I would go in such a situation. This is something you should consider when you practice self-defense.

In the following situations, I am making the assumption that you are in imminent fear for your personal safety. Your opponent has made a verbal assault, and you recognize that he is preparing to launch a physical assault. These techniques are for that moment when the opponent's hand or hands are in a relatively static position. It is always easier to defend against a static position than against a dynamic movement. These techniques make use of that moment of relative calm before an attack is launched.

Technique 31

There are seven examples of preemptive techniques described in the following section. It is always to your advantage to preplan possible responses to various situations. By practicing various scenarios, it is possible to develop a conditioned response to various stimuli, thus allowing you to respond without thought to various attacks.

Figure 31-1: You are being threatened by an opponent who is shaking his fist in your face or possibly punching you.

Figure 31-2: Deflect your opponent's hand to the left side of your head and, at the same time, punch to the solar plexus with your left fist.

Figure 31-3: As you pull back your left fist, pin your opponent's arm to your body. At the same time, use the upper portion of your right arm to apply pressure downward on your opponent's elbow.

Figure 31-4: As he is forced to the ground, there are a number of pressure points that might become targets of opportunity. Potentially you could strike the face (Conception Vessel 24 (**Figure 31a**)), the jaw (Stomach 5 (see Figure 11a)), or the side of the neck (Stomach 9 (see Figure 5b)) with your hammer fist.

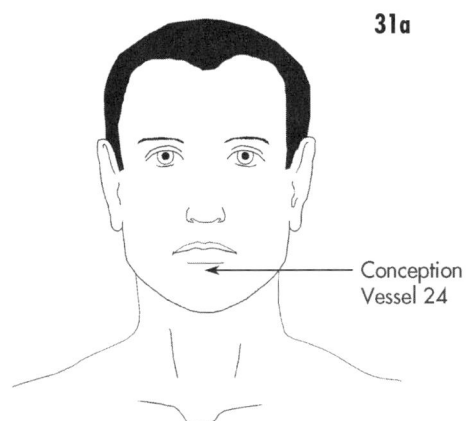

Technique 32

Figure 32–1: An individual is verbally assaulting you and shoving his finger in your face.

Figure 32–2: With your right hand, reach across your body and grab his right hand.

Figure 32–3: Punch your opponent in the side with your left hand or strike any of the points located on the side of your opponent's body.

Figure 32–4: Twist his wrist into nikyo and grab onto his right elbow with your left hand.

Figure 32–5: Push his wrist toward his elbow and rotate his wrist, attempting to position his fingers toward his head. Your right hand will press down toward your right knee, and your left hand can pull back toward your left waist.

Technique 33

This is a variation of Technique 31. The initial situation is similar in that your opponent has his fist near your face either from a threat or a punch.

Figure 33–1: You are being threatened by an opponent who is either shaking his fist in your face or punching you.

Figure 33–2: In a reactive movement, deflect your opponent's right hand toward the center and, at the same time, punch toward the solar plexus or floating ribs of your opponent.

Figure 33–3: Press your opponent's hand down with your left hand and simultaneously bring your right forearm up to strike your opponent's nose or face. If you make contact at this point, your opponent may not be in a position to continue the technique.

Figure 33–4: If you do not make contact with your opponent's forearm, continue the movement of your right hand. Once your right fist has cleared enough space to deliver a strong hammer fist, strike to his neck.

Figure 33–5: Grab the back of his neck with your right hand and rotate your opponent toward your center. At the same time, push your opponent's arm toward his center and then to the top of his head. This will cause his arm to lock out in position and allow you greater leverage in the technique.

Preemptive Techniques   97

Technique 34

When your opponent puts his hand near your face in a threatening gesture, it provides you with an opportunity to respond with an appropriate technique. One thing to consider about such situations is that your opponent has created an opportunity for you by moving a part of his body into your range of defense. You can begin to control the situation without having to move closer.

Figure 34-1: Your opponent has raised his fist and is shaking it in your face, threatening you with physical harm.

Figure 34-2: Grab your opponent's left wrist with your right hand. At the same time, punch your opponent in the solar plexus with your left fist.

Figure 34-3: Bring your left hand back toward your body and pin his arm to your chest. Release the grip on his wrist with your right hand.

Figure 34-4: Strike down on his chest with your right hammer fist and maintain pressure on his arm with your left arm.

Technique 35

This technique is similar to the technique demonstrated in Figures 34–1 through 34–4. However, the main difference is the target area you are attacking has changed because of the arm position of your opponent.

Figure 35–1: You are being threatened by an opponent who is shaking his fist in your face, or possibly punching you.

Figure 35–2: Deflect your opponent's hand to the left side of your head and simultaneously punch to his solar plexus with your left fist.

Figure 35–3: As you pull back your left fist, pin your opponent's arm to your body and use the upper portion of your right arm to apply pressure downward on your opponent's elbow.

Figure 35–4: As he is forced to the ground, strike his face, his jaw, or the side of his neck with your hammer fist.

100 75 Down Blocks

Technique 36

In the following situation, you make use of body shifting to help defend against your opponent. This type of motion can be seen in various forms when you turn.

Figure 36–1: Your opponent jabs at your face with his right hand.

Figure 36–2: Deflect his hand away from your body with your left hand. At the same time, punch your opponent in the side of his face or any target of opportunity.

Figure 36–3: With your left hand, push your opponent's arm toward his rear section, and place your right hand on the back of his neck. Of course, this could be a strike to the back of the neck, as well.

Figure 36–4: Extend your opponent's right arm and press his head down and toward your center.

Figure 36–5: Continued pressure on your opponent's head and arm will cause him to fall to the ground.

Technique 37

The following sequence of movements illustrates how you can use various parts of the "down block" movement to strike your opponent with various parts of your body. In addition, please notice how a variety of pressure points could be attacked in this example.

Figure 37-1: Your opponent threatens you with his right fist.

Figure 37-2: With your left hand, punch your opponent in the floating rib area (Liver 13 (**Figure 37a**), Spleen 16 (**Figure 37b**)) or any other target of opportunity. At the same time, punch your opponent in the side of the jaw or neck with your right hand. Targets that would be effective are Stomach 9 (see Figure 5b), Stomach 5 (see Figure 11a), Triple Warmer 17 (**Figure 37c**), or similar points.

Figure 37-2a: This shows you the technique from the other side. This shows how you should follow through with your right-hand punch and bring your hand back toward your left side, as if you were chambering a down block. By driving your left hand into the floating rib area of your opponent, you should be able to get him to bend over his right front leg.

Figure 37–3: Follow through with your right-hand punch and bring your hand back toward your left side, as if you were chambering a down block. By driving your right hand into your opponent's side, you should be able to get him to bend over his right front leg. As you retract your left hand toward your waist, clip your opponent with the knuckles of your left fist on Triple Warmer 17. Strike down with your right fist to targets of opportunity such as Gall Bladder 25 (**Figure 37d**) or Gall Bladder 26 (**Figure 37e**).

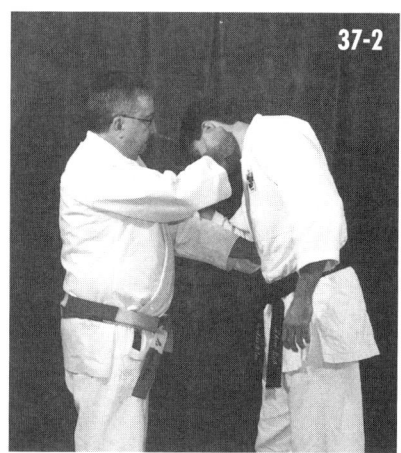

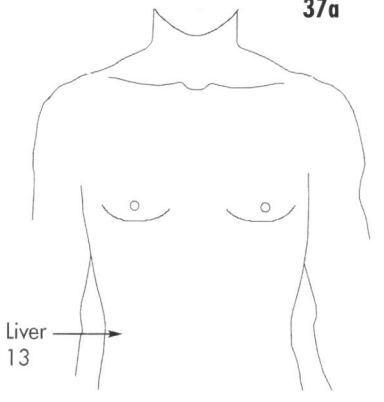

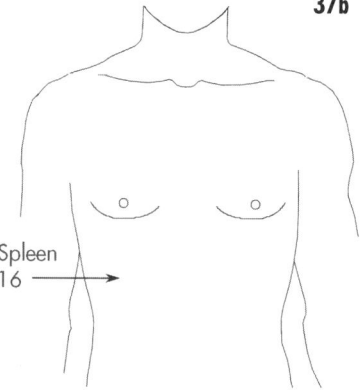

104 75 Down Blocks

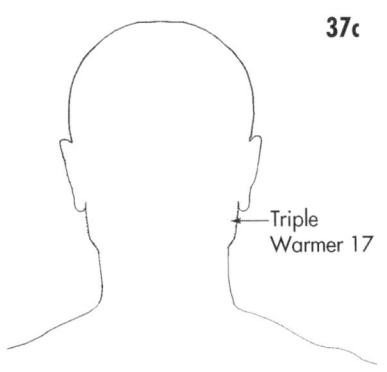

37c

Triple Warmer 17

37-2a

37-3

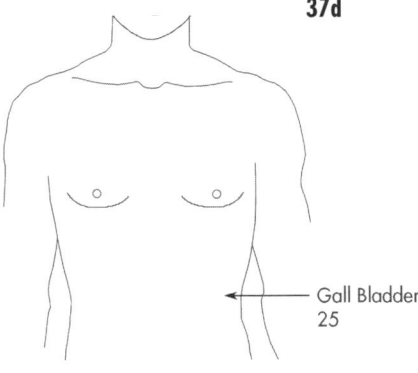

37d

Gall Bladder 25

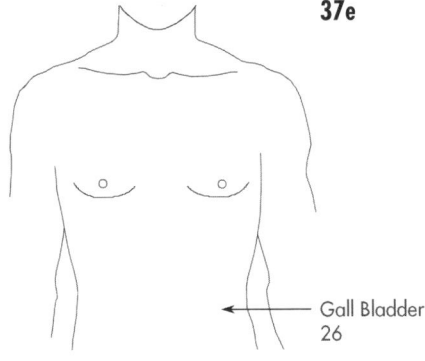

37e

Gall Bladder 26

 # Defense Against a Push

Many times when an individual wishes to intimidate you he will push you with either one or two hands. This can be a way to gauge your reaction or to build up courage for a more serious assault. It is useful, therefore, to have a number of responses prepared if you are assaulted by a push. Another important reason to practice defensive tactics against a push is that a push may come at a slower speed than a punch. This gives you the opportunity to build up your confidence in the technique as well as develop coordination. As your speed, coordination, and reflexes develop you can increase the speed of the push. In the following section, there will be eight examples of defenses against pushes.

Technique 38

Initially, you can practice a single-hand push from a greater distance, as in the following example. Once your opponent gets within arm's reach you should have your hands raised in a defensive position.

Figure 38–1: In this sequence, your opponent pushes toward your upper chest or face with his right hand.

Figure 38–2: Cover your face with your left hand and, at the same time, deflect the forward movement of his hand with your right hand.

Figure 38–3: Grab the top of his right wrist with your right hand. Simultaneously, grab the top portion of his fingers with your left hand. For this technique, you will want to have your left palm facing your opponent's palm and your thumb toward the floor.

Figure 38–4: Take your opponent to the ground by pulling your right hand back toward your waist and applying pressure on your opponent's fingers with your left hand. If possible, you will want to lodge your opponent's elbow against your side to give more stability to your technique. In addition, you will be able to press back his fingers and, by blocking the movement of his elbow, increase his pain.

Defense Against a Push   107

Technique 39

In some situations, your opponent may place his hand on your chest to arrest your forward movement or to push you back. The following technique offers you an example of how to defend against such an attack.

Figure 39–1: Your opponent pushes your left upper chest with his right hand.

Figure 39–2: Move your right hand over his hand and grab the top of it. If you can, try to put your thumb between his index and middle finger. At the same time, use your left index finger to dig into Heart 2 (see Figure 26a) of his right arm.

Figure 39–3: As you pull back with your left arm, begin to step forward with your right foot and to rotate his hand in a clockwise manner, pressing his palm toward his elbow. Remember, you will want to keep his arm in a tight "S" shape.

Figure 39–4: Continue the forward motion with your right leg because this will allow you to use your body weight in the technique. Bring your left hand back toward your belt and continue the rotation on his wrist with your right hand in conjunction with the pressure toward his elbow.

Technique 40

The following technique could be used against a push to the chest or face as well as a jab to the face. Equally, this technique could be used against a push or punch to the chest.

Figure 40-1: Your opponent pushes at your face or upper chest with his left hand. Deflect the motion of his hand with your right forearm, and push his body toward his left side.

Figure 40-2: Slide your left hand under his left arm and grab near his collar. Once you have established your grip, use your right forearm to strike the side of your opponent's head.

Figure 40-3: Maintain your grip on your opponent's collar and strike back to the side of your opponent's head with the upper portion of your right arm.

Figure 40-4: With the downward motion of your right arm, force your opponent's upper body away from you, and pull back on his collar with your left hand. This will choke him, and if you apply this technique correctly, he should pass out in thirty seconds or less. Anytime you practice a choke hold you should do it under proper supervision.

Technique 41

In the following technique, your opponent has pushed your chest and is prepared to deliver a punch to your face. By deflecting the opponent's left hand toward the midline you turn his body in such a way as to reduce his opportunity to successfully deliver a punch to your face.

Figure 41-1: Your opponent pushes the upper-right side of your body with his left hand as he threatens to punch you with his right hand.

Figure 41-2: Deflect your opponent's left hand toward your center with your right hand. At the same time, bring your left hand under his arm.

Figure 41-3: Grab your opponent's wrist with your left hand and pull it toward your waist. If you can, strike your opponent's elbow with your forearm to push him forward and cause pain.

Figure 41-4: Rotate your right hand down on your opponent's arm to lock his elbow.

DEFENSE AGAINST A PUSH   111

TECHNIQUE 42

A double-handed push to your upper chest by your opponent will move your body to the rear. This technique makes use of his forward motion as you turn. If possible, you should strive to have your body move in such a manner that you do not take any of the impact of his push, but rather smoothly receive the force and redirect the power of your opponent.

Figure 42–1: Your opponent begins to push your chest with both hands.

Figure 42–2: As your opponent pushes your chest, press your palms on his wrists from the outside inward.

Figure 42–3: Allow your body to move backward slightly with the extension of your opponent's push, maintaining contact with his wrists.

Figure 42–4: Step back with your left foot as you pivot on your right foot. At the same time, release the pressure on your opponent's right wrist and roll your left hand over the top of his left wrist.

Figure 42–5: Strike back with your right elbow as you extend your left hand in a downward motion.

Figure 42–6: Punch forward with your right hand so that you make contact at your opponent's elbow with your upper arm. This technique will either throw your opponent forward or perhaps snap his elbow.

Technique 43

This technique makes use of the principle of beating your opponent to the punch. Your opponent is attempting to push you, while you take the initiative with this technique.

Figure 43–1: Your opponent begins to push your chest with both hands.

Figure 43–2: Immediately punch your opponent's jaw with your left hand and, at the same time, deflect his left hand with your right.

Figure 43–3: As you pull your left hand back toward your body, grab your opponent's left wrist. Extend your right arm over the top of your opponent's arm.

Figure 43–4: Apply pressure downward on his elbow with your right upper arm.

Figure 43–5: If you keep pressure on his arm with the upper portion of your arm, you can use your elbow as a pivot point and strike the side of his face or neck with your right hammer fist.

Technique 44

By blending with your opponent's attack, you can step forward and apply this technique. By using your right hand to come up and under your opponent's left hand, you are able to deflect the push to your right side. Allow your opponent to push your left shoulder and continue his movement to complete this technique.

Figure 44–1: As your opponent pushes your chest with both hands, turn your body to a 45-degree angle by stepping forward with your right foot. Allow your left shoulder to absorb the push.

Figure 44–2: At the same time, move your right hand up and under your opponent's left arm.

Figure 44-3: With your right hand, push your opponent and grab his lapel. Use your left hand to guide his right arm in front of your chest, and push his lower back forward to make him lose his balance.

Figure 44-4: Pull back with your right hand, and maintain your grip on his lapel. Slide your right hand to his lower-right lapel and secure a strong grip.

Figure 44-5: Extend your right leg forward and push your knee into his lower back or side. Pull your right hand back toward your waist—your radial bone should be used to choke your opponent—and pull your left hand toward your waist. This will give you a very strong and secure choke hold on your opponent.

TECHNIQUE 45

The last of the pushing techniques makes use of preemption as well as another basic principle. It is much easier to push your opponent's hands and arms into his center line than to take his arms and move them to the outside. Once you successfully cross your opponent's arms, you have gained a momentary advantage.

Figure 45–1: Your opponent pushes toward your upper chest with both hands.

Figure 45–2: As his hands come toward your chest, push his left hand over the top of his right arm. Once his arms cross, press down on your opponent's left wrist so that it makes contact with the top of his right elbow.

Figure 45–3: Apply pressure and quickly switch your hands so that you are pulling his left wrist down with your left hand.

Figure 45–3a: This shows you a view from the opposite direction.

Figure 45–4: With your right hand, push his right wrist in such a way as to lock just above his left elbow.

Figure 45–5: Pull your left hand back toward your waist and, at the same time, press your right hand down toward your right leg.

Defense Against a Push   117

Defense Against a Single-Hand Lapel Grab

In the following section, there are six different defenses against a single-hand grab to the lapel. This is likely to be one of the most common grabs you will encounter in a self-defense situation. As with any single-hand grab, you should expect your opponent to be ready to attack you with his opposite hand.

Technique 46

This technique relies on your ability to lock your opponent's elbow and cause pain to that joint. In practice, you must be careful about the amount of pressure you apply to the elbow joint. In a self-defense situation, you would apply the technique with a sharp movement to increase the amount of pain. In such a situation, the possibility of breaking the elbow or injuring the surrounding structure of the elbow must be considered.

Figure 46-1: Your opponent grabs your right lapel with his left hand.

Figure 46-2: Turn your body slightly to help straighten his arm. At the same time, extend your left arm under your opponent's arm.

Figure 46-3: Raise your left arm so as to lock his elbow. This action will also cause your opponent's left hand to be pressed against your chest.

Figure 46-4: Step toward your left while turning your body in the same direction and, keeping contact with your opponent's elbow, sweep your left arm toward the ground. This technique can throw your opponent or cause intense pain with a lock to the elbow. If delivered with enough speed, power, and focus you could break your opponent's arm.

Technique 47

Figure 47-1: From a same-side lapel grab, your opponent attacks with his left hand.

Figure 47-2: Use the tip of your left thumb to press into Heart 2 (see Figure 26a). At the same time, reach over the top of your opponent's left hand and grab his hand. Using thumb pressure to Heart 2 causes an intense amount of pain in the majority of people. For many, you would not even need to continue with the wrist throw, because the thumb pressure alone can put them on their knees.

Figure 47-3: Step forward with your right foot, and twist your opponent's left hand in a counterclockwise manner to put him off-balance.

Figure 47-4: Continue the motion of your hands to throw your opponent to the ground.

Defense Against a Single-Hand Lapel Grab

Technique 48

In a self-defense situation such as this, it is likely that your opponent will attempt to strike you in the face. Knowing this in advance, you can practice various defensive techniques, such as this one.

Figure 48-1: Your opponent, who is preparing to deliver a punch to your face, has grabbed your left lapel.

Figure 48–2: Grab your opponent's elbow or jacket and pull him arm toward your center. Pulling your opponent sharply can slightly unbalance him as he attempts to punch your face. Deflect his punch with your left hand.

Figure 48–3: Continue to pull your opponent's right elbow past your centerline and toward your right hip.

Figure 48–4: Strike across your opponent's throat with your forearm in a downward motion. This can throw him backward.

Technique 49

In many of the traditional forms, you will find a down block followed immediately by a punch or reverse punch. In the following technique, you make use of the reverse punch to finish your defensive technique.

Figure 49-1: Your opponent grabs your right lapel and attempts to strike you in the face with his right hand. Deflect his punch toward your right side with your left hand.

Figure 49-2: Press his arm down upon his own forearm, if possible, just above the elbow.

Figure 49-3: Maintain pressure on your opponent's arm and lock it over the top of his arm. At the same time, prepare to strike your opponent with your right fist.

Figure 49-4: Punch the side of his jaw at Stomach 5 (see Figure 11a) or to the side of his neck at Stomach 9 (see Figure 5b) with your right fist.

Technique 50

Once again, you will attempt to take advantage of a situation where your opponent has not yet punched with his left hand. In such a situation, your opponent may simply be trying to intimidate you.

Figure 50–1: Your opponent has grabbed your left lapel with his right hand and indicates that he will punch you with his left hand.

Figure 50–2: Place your left arm along the outside of your opponent's right arm. At the same time, punch Heart 2 (see Figure 26a) on your opponent's right arm with your right fist. Your left arm will stabilize your opponent's arm to give you a solid target to strike.

Figure 50–3: Once you have struck your opponent's arm with your right fist, continue the motion of your right hand. At the same time, circle your left hand above your opponent's right arm and begin to press it into your body with your arm. If your opponent moves forward, you can use the continuing motion of your right hand to strike his face with your right forearm.

Figure 50–4: Immediately strike with your right hand to the back or side of his neck. Stomach 9 (see Figure 5b) or Gall Bladder 20 (**Figure 50a**) are two points that could be open for such a strike.

Defense Against a Single-Hand Lapel Grab   125

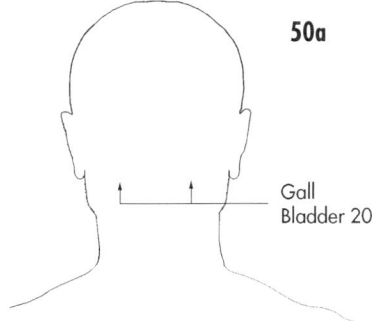

50a

Gall Bladder 20

Technique 51

In this situation, you are in extremely close proximity to your opponent. The closer you are to your opponent, the less reaction time you will have once he has initiated an attack. For this scenario, your opponent has not struck you with his fist; it is only being used to threaten you. In such a situation, the person who punches first will most likely land the first blow. It is imperative to program into your muscle memory various techniques that you can apply without thought. Although in this sequence your opponent has grabbed your lapel, it could be a grab to other areas of your upper body.

Figure 51–1: You are facing your opponent at a very close range. He has grabbed your shirt with his right hand and is threatening you with his left fist.

Figure 51–2: Grab your opponent's right arm with your left hand. At the same time, strike Heart 3 (**Figure 51a**) with your elbow. This will cause intense pain in most people and, in some cases, may cause your opponent to pass out. By placing your left hand on your opponent's arm you accomplish two goals: (1) you immobilize his arm so your strike will be effective and (2) you give yourself a target to strike. For example, close your eyes and slap your hands together. You will find this very easy, because your body knows where your hands are spatially. By holding onto your opponent you provide yourself with a similar situation—you know instinctively where your opponent's arm is, no matter if he moves it or not. Thus, you will be more likely to connect with an elbow strike in a moment of stress.

Figure 51–3: At this point, your opponent's legs will more than likely begin to buckle, and he will lose his balance toward his right-rear quadrant.

Figure 51–4: If a further technique is needed, a strike to the side of the neck or other targets of opportunity can be delivered with your right hammer fist.

Defense Against a Single-Hand Lapel Grab 127

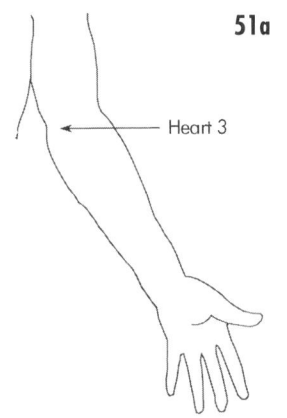

Heart 3

Defense Against a Double-Hand Grab to the Upper Body

In the following section, you will see five different attacks to the upper body that employ both of your opponent's hands. I have tried to demonstrate what I would consider to be likely methods of attack and some possible responses.

Technique 52

The following technique makes use of pulling back your right shoulder to cause your opponent to move into an unbalanced position. For maximum effectiveness with this unbalancing technique, your opponent's arm should be extended as far as possible.

Figure 52-1: Your opponent has grabbed your upper shoulder on both your right and left sides.

Figure 52-2: With your right hand, punch to the area of your opponent's navel and at the same time, bring your left arm toward the back of your opponent's neck.

Figure 52-3: As you strike the back of his neck with your left forearm, grab his belt or the top of his pants with your right hand.

Figure 52-4: Continue the forward motion of your left arm and grab your opponent's upper shoulder. If he does not have suitable clothing to grab, grab his hair.

Figure 52-5: Pull your right hand back toward your waist and simultaneously begin to move your left hand down toward your opponent's right-rear quadrant.

Figure 52-6: By continuing this motion, you will be able to throw your opponent to the ground.

Technique 53

While practicing, notice that this technique does not make use of the full range of motion of the down block; only the chambering position is utilized. This is an example of how individual portions of movements can be utilized.

Defense Against a Double-Hand Grab to the Upper Body 131

Figure 53-1: Your opponent has grabbed your lapel with both hands.

Figure 53-2: Duck your head down and in between your opponent's arms. At the same time, extend your stance and turn your body to the left.

Figure 53-3: Hook your right hand behind your opponent's knee, and shift your body weight to your rear leg.

Figure 53-4: By stepping in deep with your right foot and raising your right hand as high as you can, you should be able to sweep your opponent to the ground.

Technique 54

Dropping your body weight below your opponent's elbow allows you to make use of body shifting to maximize your strength in this technique. In addition, when you turn your body slightly to the side, you will be able to redirect the force of your opponent's right hand so that it will pass by your face.

Figure 54-1: Your opponent has grabbed your upper collar with both hands.

Figure 54-2: Grab your opponent's sleeve with your left hand and roll your knuckles into his arm, just above the elbow.

Figure 54-3: If you apply this with force, it should cause enough discomfort that your opponent will straighten his arm.

Figure 54-4: At the top of your movement, roll your left arm over the top of your opponent's arm and apply pressure downward. It is likely that, at this point, he will retain his grip on your collar.

Figure 54-5: Continued pressure on his arm will force him to the ground. If you wish to retain control over your opponent, grab his right wrist with your right hand and continue to put pressure on his arm or switch to another joint lock.

Defense Against a Double-Hand Grab to the Upper Body

Technique 55

If your opponent attempts to make use of a bear hug, you are at a tremendous advantage if you can keep your arms from being encircled. Even if you manage to keep only one hand free, you will find it possible to perform this technique.

Figure 55–1: In this example, your opponent grabs you from the front in a bear hug that does not encircle your arms.

Figure 55–2: Punch the side of his back with your left hand, and then grab his clothing in the same area. At the same time, strike Gall Bladder 20 (see Figure 50a) with your right fist or forearm.

Figure 55–3: Grab his hair with your right hand or, if he has very short hair, grab his ear.

Figure 55–4: Pull your right hand down toward your right leg. This will twist your opponent's head and allow you to throw him. Pull your left hand to your waist to give added twisting motion to the technique. You will notice that the sleeve is being used. You can maintain your grip on your opponent's side, as shown in Figure 55–3, or grab your opponent's arm again. Either approach will work quite well for throwing your opponent.

Technique 56

This technique is difficult because of the timing and body shifting required to make it work. However, it is a good technique to practice to develop a feel for body shifting and absorbing your opponent's forward pressure.

Figure 56-1: Your opponent grabs you around the waist in an attempt to wrestle you to the ground.

Figure 56-2: Grab his belt (or pants) with your right hand. At the same time, place your left hand on your opponent's elbow.

Figure 56-3: Drop your center of balance straight down and pivot toward your right side. Pull your left hand back toward your waist and begin to sweep your right hand to the side.

Figure 56-4: Throw your opponent by completing your pivot and the sweep of your right hand.

Figures 56-5 and 56-6: These figures demonstrate the movement of your body in accomplishing the throw. It is possible to accomplish this throw without the use of your hands if your opponent has committed to his movement.

136 75 Down Blocks

Defense Against a Grab from the Rear

There are seven techniques to be explored in the following section. With attacks from the rear, you will not be able to see your opponent approach and will have to react in a very spontaneous and natural manner. It is therefore important to practice various scenarios for such attacks.

Technique 57

The initial move of this technique is very simple and should be drilled until it becomes an automatic response. It is virtually impossible for an attacker to raise your arms and place you in a full nelson if you turn your thumbs to the rear. If you wish to get a feeling for how this technique works, simply turn your thumbs to the rear and try to raise your arms to the side. You will find your arms lock out, and it is very difficult to raise them very high unless you have a great deal of flexibility in your shoulder joints.

Figure 57–1: Your opponent grabs you from the rear and starts to apply a full nelson. As soon as you feel your opponent start the technique, rotate your fingers so the back of your hand is facing your side. You can bend your arms slightly and apply a small amount of force downward. By doing this your opponent will find it almost impossible to raise your arms over your head.

Figure 57–2: Press your arms down to lock your opponent's arms in position. Hold him in this position for a split second while you reach across your body and grab your opponent's fingers with your right hand.

Figure 57–3: Once the grip is secured, turn your body toward your opponent and place your left hand on top of his left elbow. Begin to force your opponent to the ground by twisting his wrist.

Figure 57–4: Once your opponent is on his knees, strike the side of his head with your left hand. You could also strike Triple Warmer 17 (see Figure 37c), Stomach 9 (see Figure 5b), Gall Bladder 20 (see Figure 50a), or any other point that presents itself as a target of opportunity.

Defense Against a Grab from the Rear

Technique 58

The following technique could be useful when an opponent grabs your shoulder from the rear and attempts to pull you backward or arrest your forward movement.

Figure 58-1: In this situation, your opponent has grabbed your right shoulder from the rear with his right hand.

Figure 58–2: Turn to face your opponent and, at the same time, grab his right hand with your left hand. As you bring your right hand back to your hip, grab your opponent's elbow from underneath.

Figure 58–3: Continue to pull his elbow back toward your waist and turn his right wrist as you would with *koto-gashi* (wrist throw).

Figure 58–4: Pull your right hand back to your waist, and your left hand will go down toward your left knee to throw your opponent.

Technique 59

Turning your body adds a great deal of power to this technique. It is important to consider how body movement and position can increase the overall effectiveness of any technique.

Figure 59–1: Your opponent has grabbed both of your upper arms from the rear.

Figure 59–2: As you turn in a counterclockwise fashion, place your right hand on top of your opponent's left hand. Begin to raise your left arm in a circular manner.

Figure 59–3: Maintain your grip on your opponent's left hand (keep it tight on your arm) and rotate your left arm above your opponent's left wrist. This should cause his wrist to bend.

Figure 59–4: Keep applying pressure on your opponent's wrist and take him to the ground.

Figure 59–4a This is another view of the technique. Notice how your grip on your opponent's hand is on the top of his fingers. This allows you to pull them back toward his body in order to make a sharper angle in the wrist and increase his pain.

Technique 60

There are two important points to consider when practicing this technique. The first is how to drop your elbows the moment your opponent grabs your wrists. This movement, combined with the sinking of your hips, allows you to perform this technique with a minimum amount of strength.

Figure 60–1: Your opponent has grabbed both of your wrists from the rear.

Figure 60–2: Circle your hands forward as you drop your center of balance down.

Figure 60-3: Step under your opponent's right arm and grab his palm with your left hand. This position would be similar to the chambering of your hand for a down block.

Figure 60-4: Apply sankyo to your opponent. You can get a great deal of pain compliance from your opponent if your grip concentrates on the area of his little finger and you keep his wrist as straight as possible. You want to turn his wrist in toward his body for the maximum amount of pain compliance.

Notice how you are grabbing the fingers of your opponent at the initial point of the technique. By grabbing your opponent's fingers, you are grabbing a weaker point of the hand and will be required to use a lesser amount of strength to initiate the control technique. You can exert a greater amount of pain by bending your opponent's little finger back and over the top of his ring finger. In addition, it may be possible to press Large Intestine 4 (see Figure 17a) with the thumb of your left hand. Sankyo is also demonstrated in Technique 17.

Figure 60-5: If you complete the downward motion of your left hand, your opponent's head will be brought close to your body. At this point, you could punch the side of his neck or face.

Technique 61

This technique makes use of the same basic body shift and elbow movement as Technique 60. In this sequence, you can see the side view of the body shift and elbow movement.

Figure 61-1: Your opponent grabs both of your wrists from the rear.

Figure 61-2: Lower your center of balance and rotate your hands forward in a circular motion.

Figure 61-3: Step back with your left foot and raise your right hand as if to chamber your down block.

Defense Against a Grab from the Rear   145

Figure 61-4: Place the knife-edge portion of your hand just above your opponent's elbow and grab his left wrist with your left hand.

Figure 61-5: Press or strike down with your right hand on top of your opponent's arm for a lock.

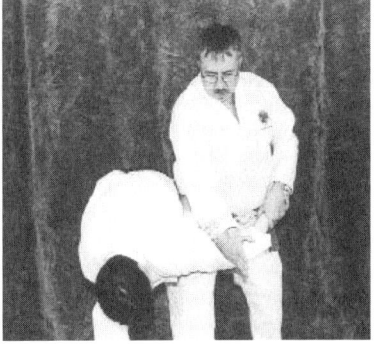

Technique 62

This sequence of movement is a continuation of Technique 61. Notice that the end position of Figure 61–5 is similar to Figure 62–1; however, the hand position is reversed. In this sequence, the intent is to show how the down block motion can be used as a reversal if your opponent attempts to counter your arm bar.

Figure 62–1: You have applied an arm bar on your opponent.

Figure 62–2: He is able to bend his arm into a position to begin to turn his back toward you.

Figure 62–3: In an attempt to escape the lock, your opponent delivers an elbow strike toward your face. Because the elbow to the face is likely to be used, you should be prepared to counter this strike with your left arm.

Figure 62–4: Using your left forearm, deflect the movement up. Be sure to maintain your grip on his left wrist with your right hand.

Figure 62–5: Sweep your left hand downward and pull your right hand back toward your waist.

Figure 62–6: This will put your opponent in a very unbalanced position where other techniques can be applied.

Defense Against a Grab from the Rear 147

Technique 63

It is hard to convey in words and pictures, but when doing this technique do not attempt to pull away from your opponent with strength from your wrist area. Instead, concentrate on body shifting and the force being used from your elbow. Your hand should follow the push from your elbow.

Figure 63–1: In this sequence, your opponent has grabbed your arm and is attempting to apply an arm bar.

Figure 63–2: Turn back toward your opponent and chamber your left hand, which should pull your opponent in slightly toward your body.

Figure 63–3: At the same time, punch with your right hand to the solar plexus or around the navel. Notice how this can be seen as the first half of the down block movement.

Figure 63–4: Reach back with your right hand and grab your opponent's wrist to disengage his grip.

Figure 63–5: As you pull back with your right hand, strike your opponent in the groin or lower stomach with your left hammer fist.

DEFENSE AGAINST A GRAB FROM THE REAR   149

TECHNIQUE 64

In this technique, if you try to pull your wrist away from your opponent you will have to use superior muscle strength. However, if you press your arm in toward your opponent, allow your wrist to drop, then press your elbow toward your opponent's stomach, you will find that this technique does not require a great deal of strength.

Figure 64–1: In this sequence, your opponent has grabbed your arm and is trying to apply an arm bar.

Figure 64–2: Do not pull with your wrist; rather, push with your body, led by your elbow, toward the center of your opponent.

Figure 64–3: Grab the sleeve of your opponent at the elbow with your left hand. Do not try to pull your right hand away from your opponent, but rotate your palm toward your face as if to chamber the down block.

Figure 64–4: Pull your right hand back toward your waist and begin to apply pressure to the little-finger area of your opponent's hand. As you apply pressure rotate your palm so that it faces away from the center of your body.

Figure 64–4a: This gives you a closer view of the lock.

Figure 64–5: Continue both the pressure on the elbow and the rotation of your opponent's wrist. This will cause him to fall to the ground, where you will be able to continue with a control technique if you desire.

75 Down Blocks

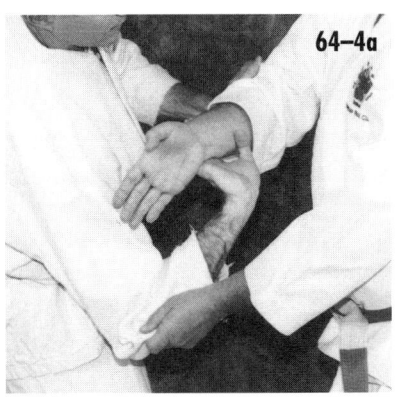

# DEFENSE AGAINST A PUNCH

In the following four examples, there are four techniques used to defend against a punch. Defending yourself against a punch is more difficult than doing so against a grab or push, because the punch is delivered faster and with greater power. Another consideration is a punch is normally retracted quickly. A grab presents a more stationary target for your counterattack. You should also remember that, if contact is made with a punch, it can cause damage, whereas the grab or push is not likely to cause any injury.

Technique 65

In a situation where you have the opportunity to raise your hands in a defensive position, you stand a better chance of defending yourself against an attack. One consideration in preparing a defense can be the position of your hands. If you have your arms wide, it presents an opportunity for your opponent to jab toward your face. If you keep your hands and arms closer, you close out the jab, but offer an opportunity for your opponent to use a hook punch. Being aware of probable angles of attack can help you prepare to defend yourself against an attack.

Figure 65–1: Close to you, your opponent has his hands up to attack with a punch or is actually striking.

Figure 65–2: Strike across your body with your right hand into the area of your opponent's elbow. If possible, you could target Lung 5 (see Figure 12a) to cause your opponent's legs to buckle and make his head turn toward his left side. This would facilitate the takedown demonstrated in this sequence.

Figure 65–3: Rotate your hand down to push your opponent to the side.

Figure 65–4: With your left hand, grab your opponent's collar and pull back toward your left side. This should sufficiently unbalance him so that you can take him to the ground.

Technique 66

At times you may not have the opportunity to raise your hands in a defensive position. In these moments you will need to develop reflexive techniques to defend yourself. The following technique makes use of a deflection and grab to off-balance your opponent.

Figure 66–1: Your opponent faces you and prepares to strike you with his right hand.

Figure 66–2: As he strikes, brush his hand away from your face with your left hand. Immediately check his arm at or above his elbow with your right hand.

Figure 66–3: Slide your right hand back along his right arm and grab his wrist. He will retract his arm once he has punched, so you should attempt to maintain contact with his arm as a way to secure your grip.

Figure 66–4: Use your left forearm to push across on his elbow and begin a lock on his arm. This should push your opponent to his left side. As you pull your opponent's right wrist to your right side, strike his exposed left side with your fist or hammer fist.

Technique 67

The distance between yourself and your opponent in this situation is much greater than in the previous examples. Because the distance is greater, you will have a bit more time to react to the initial attack of your opponent. Do not allow yourself to be complaisant; it is possible to launch an attack to your face very quickly. There are many skilled individuals who could cover the distance between you and themselves so quickly you would hardly notice the movement.

Defense Against a Punch

Figure 67–1: Your opponent prepares to punch you with his right hand.

Figure 67–2: Deflect his punch with your left hand. At the same time, punch to his side with your right hand. You could strike any number of points on the side of his body, such as Liver 13 (see Figure 37a) or Liver 14 (**Figure 67a**), Gall Bladder 23 (**Figure 67b**) or Gall Bladder 24 (**Figure 67c**), and Spleen 16 (see Figure 37b).

Figure 67–3: When you pull your right hand back to your side, push down on your opponent's right hand with your left palm to help you trap his arm. Strike to your opponent's head or neck area with your left hand.

Figure 67–4: Continue the motion of your hand and push your opponent to the ground. Lock your opponent's arm with your left arm.

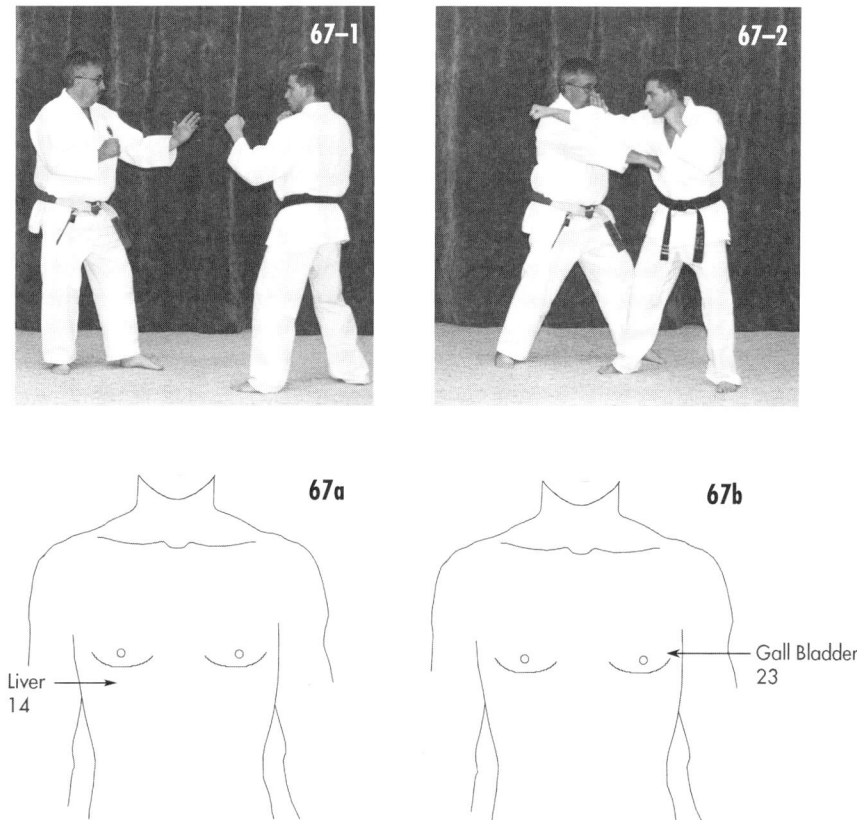

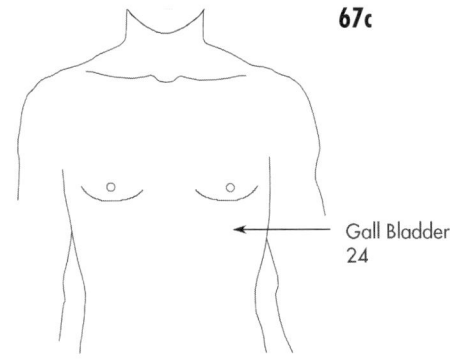

67c

Gall Bladder 24

Technique 68

From this position, it is probable your opponent will jab toward your face with his forward hand. By being aware of this it may be possible to read his intention and brush his punch to the side with your left hand.

Figure 68-1: You and your opponent are facing each other at medium range.

Figure 68-2: As your opponent jabs toward your head with his left hand, parry the punch with your left hand. At the same time, punch to his solar plexus or other body point with your right hand.

Figure 68-3: As you bring your right hand back to your side, grab your opponent's arm or sleeve to pull him into your second punch.

Defense Against a Punch 157

15 DEFENSE AGAINST A STICK

In an effort to think outside of the box, the following techniques will look at movements that offer a defense against an attack with a stick, and the use of the stick as a means to apply a countertechnique. In this section, there will be seven techniques that make use of techniques that can be found in Modern Arnis, created by Remy Presas.

Technique 69

This technique looks so simple it's hard to believe it works. During practice, if your partner is not aware of the technique you are going to perform, and he maintains a strong grip on his stick, you should be able to throw your partner without much difficulty. At the very least, you will find this is an effective stick disarm.

Figure 69–1: Your opponent faces you with a stick in a threatening gesture.

Figure 69–2: Step forward and grab the stick so that your little finger is up toward the ceiling and your palm is facing your opponent.

Figure 69–3: As you bring your hand down, twist the stick toward your opponent's left-rear quadrant. You do not want to apply the pressure directly back, toward his shoulder, but rather to the side.

Figure 69–4: If you continue the downward motion, and your opponent maintains a tight grip on the stick, it will be possible to bend his wrist in such a way as to cause him to lose his balance and be thrown. If your opponent is able to keep his arm close to his body, you will have to overcome his resistance with muscular strength. If, however, you can position his arm farther away from his body, you will have a mechanical advantage over your opponent. At this point, he will either fall to the ground or release the weapon.

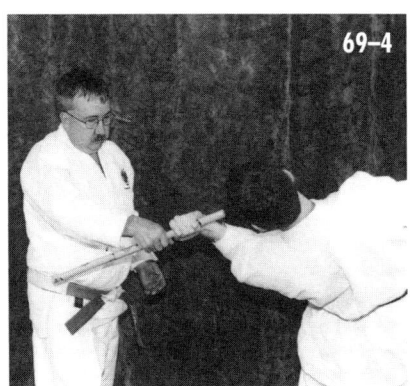

Technique 70

When defending against a stick, you can begin to determine the likely direction of the attack by the initial position of the stick.

Figure 70–1: In this sequence, your opponent has the stick in his right hand and "cocked," ready to strike. You can be almost 100 percent sure that he will swing the stick from his left to right and most likely at your upper section.

Figure 70–2: Knowing this, your body motion should be to his right side. Stop the forward motion of his arm with your left hand at his elbow.

Figure 70–3: Once you have slowed the forward momentum of the stick, grab it with your right hand.

Figure 70–4: Maintain a grip on your opponent's right elbow with your left hand, and twist the stick in such a way as to cause the "butt end" of the stick to be on top of his wrist.

Figure 70–5: You can then apply pressure to the wrist with the stick. This lock would be very similar to nikyo. The pressure should be enough to take him to the ground or disarm him. If you would like further examples of nikyo please refer to Techniques 10 and 32.

Defense Against a Stick 161

Technique 71

The following technique makes use of the stick to apply greater pressure to your opponent's elbow. Notice how in Figure 71–5 you have placed the end of the stick in the stomach of your opponent. This allows you to lock the stick in place and develop greater leverage when you press on your opponent's elbow.

Figure 71–1: Your opponent attempts to strike your upper body with a backhand strike. Strike his wrist with your right hand.

Figure 71–2: Grab onto his right wrist with your right hand. At the same time, reach under his arm and grab the stick with your right hand, palm facing up. Having your palm in this position will allow you to continue the technique without having to change your grip.

Figure 71–3: Maintain pressure on his wrist with your right hand and pull back on the stick, using it as a lever to disarm your opponent. The farther toward the end of the stick you are able to grab, the more leverage you will have for this technique, and you will be able to continue the technique without changing your grip on the stick.

Figure 71–4: Pull your right hand back toward your waist. At the same time, press on his elbow with your right fist, or the end of the stick, to extend his arm.

Figure 71–5: Once his arm is extended, slip the stick in front of your opponent's stomach and place the end of the stick nearest your hand over the top of his elbow.

Figure 71–6: Apply downward pressure on his arm for an arm bar.

DEFENSE AGAINST A STICK   163

Technique 72

This technique can be performed with a stick in your hand as well as with empty hands, as in the version demonstrated.

Figure 72-1: Your opponent attempts to thrust the stick into your stomach.

Figure 72-2: Step toward your right side and deflect the stick to your left side with the back of your forearm.

Figure 72-3: Bring your right hand up as in a chambering motion. At the same time, grab the stick near your opponent's wrist. As you bring your arm back down, strike his forearm with your elbow.

Figure 72-4: Continue to sweep your hand down and to the side and pull your left hand back toward your waist. You can twist your wrist to increase the effectiveness of the disarm. Notice that this moves your opponent's body so that his back is toward you. In this position, you can thrust the butt end of the stick into his back or kidney area.

DEFENSE AGAINST A STICK 165

TECHNIQUE 73

One of the common features of Modern Arnis is the ability to perform a technique with a stick in hand, a knife, other weapon, or empty-handed. The following example gives you a very clear idea of how this could be accomplished. Simply picture that, as the defender, you do not have a stick in your hand, and you will be able to see how this technique could be performed empty-handed.

Figure 73-1: In this sequence, both you and your opponent have sticks. Your opponent attempts a forehand strike to the upper portion of your body. Parry the strike with your stick, with the palm of your hand facing your head. This movement is similar to the chambering position of the down block.

Figure 73-2: Sweep your hand down so that your wrist is in contact with that of your opponent. While it is difficult to see, you can apply pressure to the elbow of your opponent with your left hand.

Figure 73-3: Bring your right hand back toward your waist and trap your opponent's wrist and stick at your waist. At the same time, use your left arm to apply an arm bar.

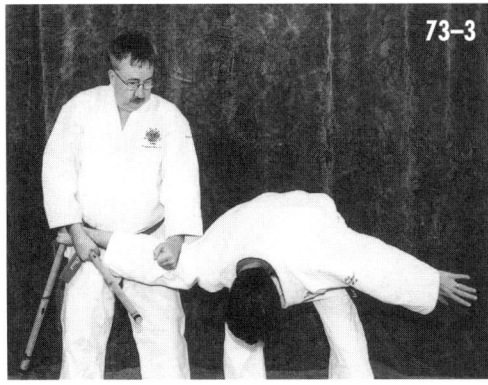

Technique 74

Weapon retention is a concern addressed in law enforcement and correctional officers' training. If you offer training to such officers, the following technique could prove to be a valuable addition to the skills you teach.

Figure 74–1: You have a stick in your right hand.

Figure 74–2: Your opponent attempts to grab it away from you using both hands. Grab the end of your stick with your left hand. At the same time, push the stick toward your left side.

Figure 74–3: Push up on the stick with your left hand and, at the same time, hook your right hand under the elbow of your opponent so that it begins to bend. This position is similar to the chambering motion of the down block.

Figure 74–4: Circle your right hand down and maintain a grip on the stick with both hands.

Figure 74–5: As your right hand comes to just above your knee your opponent will be forced to the ground. If, during the technique, you are able to grab your opponent's right hand with your left, you will be able to maintain an effective lock on your opponent.

Technique 75

The following technique is very dangerous and could break your opponent's neck. Such a break could result in your opponent's becoming a quadriplegic or even dying. Please exercise extreme care when practicing this technique.

Figure 75-1: You are in close proximity to your opponent as he attempts to strike your upper body with a stick. With your right hand strike his wrist.

Figure 75-2: Step into your opponent and, with your left hand, reach around behind his neck and grab the stick.

Figure 75-3: Using the stick as a lever, pull your opponent in toward your body. Slide your right hand from his wrist and grab the top of his right hand.

Figure 75-4: Continue to apply pressure on your opponent's neck by pulling down with your left hand.

Figure 75-5: As your left hand goes down toward your left knee, pull your right hand in toward your hip.

Appendix A

Pressure Points

Abbreviations

The following are abbreviations used in the book. These terms refer to the various acupuncture points.

GB = Gall Bladder
H = Heart
LI = Large Intestine
Liv = Liver
L = Lung
S = Stomach
Sp = Spleen
TW = Triple Warmer
CV = Conception Vessel

Location of Pressure Points

GB 20	Located in the depression between the sterno-cleido-mastoideus muscle and the trapezius. It is directly under the occipital protuberance.
GB 23	Located on a line with the nipple, and in between the 4th intercostal space.
GB 24	Located in the 7th intercostal space below Liver 14.
GB 25	Located on the side of the body, at the lower border of the end of the 12th rib.
GB 26	Located in between the ends of the 11th and 12th ribs and level with the navel.
GB 31	Located on the outside of the thigh; if you were to hang your arms loosely at your side, the tip of your middle finger would touch this point.

H 2	Located approximately 3 inches above the elbow in the groove formed by the two muscles.
L 3	Located approximately 6 inches above Lung 5 on the radial side of the biceps brachii.
L 5	Located in the cubital crease on the radial side of the tendon of the biceps brachii.
L 7	Located 1.5 inches above the transverse crease of the wrist on the radial bone. This is the point where the radial nerve becomes superficial.
LI 11	Located in the depression found at the end of the transverse cubital crease.
LI 4	Located in the middle of the 2nd metacarpal bone on the radial side.
Liv 13	Located on the end of the 11th rib.
Liv 14	Located directly below the nipple in the intercostal space of the 6th and 7th ribs.
S 5	Located midway along the side of the jaw; you can feel a slight depression there.
S 9	Located posterior to the carotid artery on the side of the sterno-cleido-mastoideus muscle, level with the Adam's apple.
Sp 21	Located in the 6th intercostal space on the midaxillary line.
Sp 6	Located the width of four fingers from the top of the ankle bone, on the back side of the tibia.
Sp 16	Located approximately halfway between the nipple and a line 4 inches to the side of the navel.
TW 13	Located at the crease at the posterior border of the deltoid muscle.
TW 17	Located just behind the earlobe in the depression found at the end of the mandible.
CV 24	Located in the depression just below the lower lip, on the center line of the body.

Appendix B

Erwin Von Baelz and the Revival of the Japanese Martial Arts

History has a fascinating way of repeating itself—or, at least, offering some interesting parallels between historical eras. For the martial artist, one of the most intriguing of these parallels has to do with two of the most critical periods in the development of the Japanese martial arts.

The first of these two eras contains the original introduction of combat forms to Japan. This story is well known:

Bodhidharma was born in Kanchi, in the southern Indian kingdom of Pallava, and was the first Patriarch of Chinese Zen Buddhism and the twenty-eighth Patriarch of Indian Buddhism.

He was the third son of King Sugandha and of the Brahmin caste. He probably would have studied the indigenous forms of combat (vajramushti) as part of his education as a royal prince. It is believed his Buddhist master, Prajnatara, instructed him to spread the word of Buddhism to China.

According to legend, Bodhidharma traveled east to southern China around 526 A.D. and is reputed to have met with Emperor Wu Ti of the Liang dynasty. However, the meeting was not to the satisfaction of either party, and Bodhidharma traveled north to the Shaolin temple at Sung Shan in the province of Honan (520 A.D.).

During his stay at the Shaolin temple, Khim & Draeger (1979) state, "Ta Mo *Bodhidharma* became disturbed over the fact the monks there frequently fell asleep during meditation. He thereupon designed special exercises by which the monks could increase their stamina and so stay their weariness" (p. 13).

Accordingly, he taught a method of conditioning called Shin Pa Lo Han Sho (Haines 1968). These basic eighteen exercises were used for improving their health and are reputed to be the foundation of the martial arts system of the famous Shaolin Temple. By his actions, Bodhidharma, this man from the West, introduced the East to a method of physical fitness based on martial arts.

On June 9, 1876, a second man, who would also come to play an important, but often underappreciated, role in the development of modern Japan, arrived in Yokohama from the West. Not only would he play a critical role in the development of the medical education system of Japan, but it can also be argued that he influenced the development of the modern Japanese martial arts. Some have credited him with the resurgence of the martial arts in Japan and their use for physical education.

This remarkable man was Dr. Erwin Baelz, who traveled to Japan to teach Western medicine at Todai (Tokyo) University. While in this position Dr. von Baelz became personal physician to the Crown Prince Yoshihito, subsequently Emperor Taisho, and many of the most important men and women in Japan. His circle of friends included the power brokers of Japan at that time.

(His influence is still felt in the medical community. In 1964 Nippon Boehringer Ingelheim Co., Ltd. initiated the Erwin von Baelz Prize to promote international collaboration between Japan and Germany in the field of medicine.)

When he started teaching he found that "the students at the Imperial University of Tokyo were badly nourished and overworked youths, who would often sit at their books all night, and took no bodily exercise, so that when examinations were at hand they often broke down and sometimes actually died of exhaustion" (Baelz 1974, p. 72).

As a professor of medicine and Privy Counselor, Baelz (Klinger-Klingerstorff 1953, p. 11) was naturally concerned with the physical condition of his students, and tried to introduce physical education to promote their health.

Baelz had arrived at a significant moment in the development of modern Japan. He stated: "In the 1870s, at the outset of the modern era, Japan went through a strange period in which she felt a contempt for all native achievements. Their own history, their own religion, their own art, did not seem to Japanese worth talking about, and or even regarded as matters to be ashamed of" (Ibid., p. 72).

After their first contacts with Western cultures, the Japanese were ashamed of their past and regarded it as a time of barbarism. One cultured man even went so far as to say of those days, "We have no history. Our history begins today" (Baelz 1974, p. 17).

To give an example of how deep these feeling must have ran, Dr. Baelz notes in his diary (November 8, 1880), "The famous 'Temple of Hachiman' still stands in the fine fir grove, though of course the trees are different. Two kilometers away is the celebrated Daibutsu, a colossal bronze statue of a seated Buddha. The face is very fine. Ten years ago the Japanese government was thinking of selling this most splendid of all the bronzes in Japan to foreigners for its price as old metal! So little veneration remains for these ancient relics. Happily, however, the negotiations came to nothing. Today the Daibutsu is treated with more respect, as a national curio" (Baelz 1974, p. 63).

This dislike of their heritage carried over to the martial arts, which were considered to be relics of the feudal past. "The native methods of bodily exercise, Japanese fencing, and jujitsu, and alike were placed under the ban. The older generation would not teach, and the younger generation would not learn, anything but European science." (Baelz, 1974, p. 72).

However, like Lafcadio Hearn (a.k.a. Koizumi Yakumo), Dr. Baelz did not want to see Japan completely abandon the traditions of its culture in favor of total Westernization. He wanted the Japanese to identify everything that was good in their cultural heritage, and then attempt to adapt it, slowly and purposively and carefully, to the changing conditions they found in their time.

He believed that the traditional martial arts could serve as a valuable way of promoting physical fitness, and proposed that students at Tokyo University begin to study kenjutsu. However, the administration discounted his idea—they felt kenjustu was a rough, and even dangerous, sport.

This position of the administration may have been influenced by the fear that students using newly developed sword-fighting skills might harm foreigners. This fear probably had some basis in reality. Just a few years before Baelz made his proposal, foreigners (as well as some native Japanese) had been attacked and killed by advocates of *sonno joi* (revere the emperor, expel the barbarian), and foreign shipping had been bombarded in the straits of Shimonoseki (Mason & Caiger 1997, p. 263).

Dr. Baelz, however, had been captivated by his first encounter with Kenjutsu. In his diary entry for Sunday, August 3, 1879, Dr. Baelz wrote about his observation of "a great fencing-match. I had heard a good deal about the sport, but this was my first sight of it, and I had the luck to witness one of the finest exhibitions given for many years" (Baelz 1974, p. 48).

He must have been highly impressed with this exhibition because he decided to become a student of fencing himself—which he saw as a way to overcome the popular conception of it as rough and dangerous:

"Not until, in order to overcome this prejudice, I myself took lessons from the most famous fencing master of the day, Sakakibara, and secured little publicity for the fact in newspapers, did interest in this old method of fencing revive."

It was felt that, if a foreigner, and, what was more, a professor of medicine at what was then the only University in the country, was studying the art, it was impossible to suppose that Westerners could regard it as "barbarous or dangerous" (Baelz 1974, p. 73).

On November 1, 1909, the first college kendo federation was formed at Tokyo University (Sasamori & Warner 1968, p. 59). It appears the Dr. Baelz's efforts to incorporate Japanese fencing into Tokyo University had finally succeeded.

Dr. Baelz also played a critical role in the introduction of jujitsu into the school curriculum. During the late 1870s he was introduced to the form while visiting the provincial capital of Chiba:

"Talking to the governor about modern education, I complained how little interest in sport of any kind were shown by well-to-do youths of the upper classes, though their health was poor, and vigorous exercise would do them a lot of good. The governor was quite inclined to my way of thinking, and expressed a strong regret that jujitsu, as a splendid method of physical training formerly much practiced in Japan, should have gone so completely out of use.

"It was, in fact, still practiced in his town, where an old teacher of the art, Totsuka by name, instructed the police in it. The results had been marvelous, and his men found it of the greatest value in making arrests. Next day, he asked me to attend a gathering where Totsuka, a man over seventy years of age, gave a demonstration of the principals of jujitsu and showed the various grips. There I watched dozens of jujitsu contests, and was extremely impressed with the results. I saw neck breaking grips and movements and throws executed without causing the least injury to the contestants, and I said to myself that this would be an ideal form of gymnastics for my students.

"Still, I had no success in the matter in Tokyo. The director of the medical school and the other leading Japanese at the University and in the Ministry for Education would not hear word of my proposal to summon the jujitsu expert from Chiba to give a demonstration in Tokyo. The students, they said, had come to the University to do mental work. There had been some sense in jujitsu in the old days, when people had to protect themselves against armed men, but that was all over now.

"My insistence that I was concerned only with jujitsu as a means of bodily training, as a matter of health, had no effect. Then it occurred to me to do what I had done in the case of the Japanese sword fencing, and arouse interest by studying jujitsu for myself. Unfortunately I cannot find any teacher willing to accept me as a pupil, for they all said that it is necessary to begin in boyhood, and I, being 30, might easily do myself serious harm" (Baelz 1974, pp. 73–74).

Eventually, according to Klinger-Klingerstorff, Dr. Baelz did in fact take "a course under one of the oldest masters, the 70-year-old Totsuka" (Klinger-Klingerstorff 1953, p. 11).

Dr. Baelz's exploration of the martial arts didn't stop with kendo and jujitsu. As he wrote in his diary on December 14, 1879, "I am now diligently trying to master the art of Japanese archery. The bow is a very stout one, so that it is a hard job to string it. I have had a platform [for practice] built on the roof of my house" (Baelz 1974, p. 54).

As noted earlier, Baelz's interest in the martial arts started with his concern over the physical condition of the students at the University.

Baelz would have been familiar with the rigors of university life in Germany, and his interest in physical fitness would have been influenced by two traditions current in the university culture in Germany at that time: the Turnverein movement, and the tradition of student dueling.

While still in Germany, Baelz had joined "Die Germanen" (literally, "The Germans"), which was a Turnerschaft corps that still followed the traditional Greater German ("Grossdeutschen") corps ideas (Bälz 1931, p.15).[1]

As a member of a Turnerschaft, Baelz would have been fully conversant with the ideas of Friedrich Jahn, who had founded the Turnverein movement in Berlin in 1811. Germany at that time was a state that had been humiliated by Napoleon, and Jahn hoped to "supply his country with a body of young men inspired by patriotism and love for freedom, men who, at the call to arms, would willingly sacrifice their lives to liberate Germany from the tyranny of a foreign rule" (Metzner 1987, p. 37).

This program would have fit very nicely with the attitudes of the Japanese of the time.

Before Baelz traveled to Japan, Jahn's philosophy had made its way to America. Three of Jahn's disciples played important roles in the spread of physical education in the United States. Carl Beck, Carl Follen, and Francis Lieber all fled Germany, and, starting in the mid-1820s, introduced Jahn's system of physical training into colleges and universities across America. Carl

Beck, along with J.G. Cogswell and George Bancroft, established a boys' school at Round Hill in Northampton, Massachusetts, where the first gymnasium in America, based on Jahn's ideas, was started.

Carl Follen was an active teacher at Round Hill until 1826, when he accepted a position at Harvard as a professor of church history (he later taught German language and literature). Follen established the second gymnasium in America at Harvard. Lieber founded a "swimming school in Boston where John Quincy Adams, President of the United States, paid a personal visit" (Metzner 1987, p. 47). During the Civil War in America Lieber became "an intimate advisor of the administration on questions of military and international law" (Ibid., p. 47).

The "Turners" of America made a lasting impression on the educational system of the United States. As a direct result of the Turners' work, physical education was introduced into the public school system of Indianapolis, Indiana. In 1907, Indianapolis was chosen as the new home for the Normal College of the American Gymnastic Union, which was the collegiate training school of the North American Turnerbund. The courses they offered for physical education teachers helped establish physical education in schools throughout the United States.

As a member of the Turnerschaft and a physician, Baelz would have been familiar with the Turners' philosophy of physical fitness and health. It is inconceivable that Baelz would have not have followed the work of other followers of Jahn with great interest and pride. Indeed, Baelz would have been extremely interested in emulating and replicating the success of the other members of the Turnverein during his stay in Japan.

Baelz also probably had more than a passing knowledge of dueling, as practiced in the German universities of that time. While Baelz was studying to become a physician, he would have been aware of the duels fought among the students, army officers, and members of the upper class. Clearly, as a former member of the Army, a University student and a member of the nobility, he would have had plenty of opportunities to observe the dueling practices of the time.

Dueling played an important role throughout German culture—a man defended his honor by dueling. "Members of the upper echelon of society were members of the dueling fraternities and doctors and jurists in the civilian duelists were most prominent" (McAleer 1997, p. 149). Fencing, which was firmly established in the German universities by the sixteenth century, can trace its roots to the late Middle Ages, when fencing was taught in the universities of France and Italy.

As a member of the upper classes, you would have been expected to be prepared to duel so that the honor of yourself—and your class—could be upheld. "Among German males, in order to be considered *salongfähig*—fit for good society—it was necessary that one also be *satisfaktionsfähig*—capable of dispensing satisfaction in a duel" (McAleer 1997, pp. 2–4).

The Japanese that Baelz encountered in his new teaching position would have shared these ideas—of honor and the use of the sword for purposes of dueling. This shared value is demonstrated by Tomofusa Sasa, a Japanese man in Germany, who in 1897 wrote a letter back to Japan about a student duel he observed in a German university that said "my poor pen is incapable of describing how impressed I was with this brave spectacle" (McAleer 1997, p. 119).

It's important to realize that Dr. von Baelz didn't change Japanese attitudes toward the martial arts and physical fitness all by himself. Without the help of prominent local proponents of the traditional martial arts, von Baelz might not have achieved the same level of success. Japanese martial arts instructors, especially, matched Baelz's support for the revival of their disciplines.

Sasamori and Warner (1968) credit Kenkchi Sakakibara (1830–1894) for having "aroused and fostered interest among the people by sponsoring fencing exhibitions for a small admission fee." Sakakibara had received permission from the government to conduct fencing exhibitions. The first of these was held in Asakusa, Tokyo, on April 11, 1873 (Ibid., p. 58). "Such efforts were the starting point for the revival of kendo schools in the latter part of the Meiji period" (Ibid., p. 57).

By 1887, a fencing demonstration was given at the residence of Prince Fushimi, where Sakakibara demonstrated splitting a helmet with a sword in the presence of the Emperor Meiji (Ibid., p. 58).

(While I cannot state definitively that this was the same Sakakibara from whom Baelz took fencing lessons, it does seem likely. The records of Sakakibara's fencing school show that foreigners did study fencing with him at Kurumazaka in Tokyo.)

Other kendo masters of the time who wanted to keep the practice of fencing alive supported the "Sword Unit of the Tokyo police force. The Metropolitan Police Bureau at one time had 6,000 members in this special force. The bureau strongly encouraged the continued practice of kendo and judo among the members of its organization" (Ibid., p. 57).

Von Baelz reported that Professor Jigoro Kano and his followers were responsible for convincing the administration of Tokyo University to invite Totsuka—the leading teacher of the time—to the University for a jujitsu contest.

Unfortunately, it appears Kano and his students lacked the skill to overcome their opponents from Chiba. The results of this match "made it clear how much training is needed to learn the art, for of all the young men who had been working at it in Tokyo, not one, not even Kano, could cope with the police officers who had been trained by Totsuka in Chiba" (Baelz 1974, p. 74).

Another decisive turning point in the development of judo came in 1886, when the Tokyo Metropolitan Police Board arranged a tournament between the schools of Kano and Totsuka. It was a decisive battle in which both schools picked fifteen men to represent their art. This time, the group from the Kodokan won all of the points except for two, which ended in a draw (Kodokan 1963, p. 5).

Dr. Baelz may also not have been the only European influence on Jigoro Kano's work. In 1906, in addition to a standard syllabus, judo adopted a standard dogi (Stevens 1995, p. 41). The dogi established by Kano may have been based on the traditional garb of Japan—or it may have been based on the clothing used in the wrestling style of Cornwall and Devon (in the UK). Both of these styles of wrestling required the contestants to "wear loose jackets and take holds only above the waist or on any part of the jacket" (James et al. 1946, p. 400). A decision was based on the winner's throwing his opponent so that the following three points touched: two shoulders and a hip or both hips and a shoulder. This type of "scoring" is very similar to the "ippon" or full point given in judo contests (Ibid., p. 400).

This Western style of wrestling was popular in the early 1800s, and it is conceivable that Professor Kano may have been exposed to it through his study of books on Western wrestling. It has been said that Professor Kano developed "katagruma" in 1877 through his research on Western wrestling in the Tokyo Library.

For example, many techniques similar to those of jujitsu were demonstrated in *Klare Onderrichtinge der Voortreffelijcke Worstel-Konst* by Romein de Hooghe, published in 1674. For example, it includes a version of the throw we now know as tomenage, or stomach throw.

In 1889, Professor Kano was asked to tour educational institutions in Europe at the request of the Imperial Household Agency. He didn't return to Japan until 1891. It is clear that Professor Kano had the opportunity to be strongly influenced not only by wrestling styles of the United Kingdom but by those of Germany as well. The part played by outside forces can only be speculated upon, but there is ample evidence to support a connection to European influences.

Dr. von Baelz's enthusiasm for the uniquely Japanese martial arts is even more amazing given the context. As an eminent Professor of Medicine at Tokyo University, as well as the physician for the Imperial family, Dr. Baelz seems like an unlikely candidate to take up the study of three traditional Japanese martial arts—judo/jujitsu, kyudo, and kenjutsu—just as they reached a low point in popularity among the Japanese public in the late 1870s!

Consider that most of the "old masters" of Japanese and Okinawan martial arts were not even born at this time, or were very young! For example: Morihei Ueshiba (1883–1969), Hironori Ohtsuka (1892–1982), Genwa Nakasone (1886–1978), Kori Kudaka (1907–1988), Masaru Sawayama (1906–1977), Tatsu Yamada (1905–1967), Anbun Tokuda (1886–1945), Shimpan Gusukuma (1890–1954), Hohan Soken (1889–1982), Juhatsu Kiyoda (1886–1967), and Chojun Miyagi (1888–1953). Chotoku Kyan (1870–1945) would have been around nine years old at this time! (McCarthy 1999).

To look at it from another perspective—the first section of railroad track, covering a total of 18.08 miles between Yokohama and Tokyo, was opened in 1872. By 1884, there were only 76.06 miles of railroad track in all of Japan (Mason & Caiger 1997, p. 273)! This is the environment in which Dr. Baelz began his attempt to revive the traditional Japanese martial arts!

That Baelz had considerable influence over the rejuvenation of the martial arts in Japan is without question. Certainly, those in political power took Dr. Baelz seriously, because of his close ties with the Imperial family, if nothing else. Dr. Baelz's and Dr. Kano's efforts to introduce kenjutsu and judo into Tokyo University were eventually rewarded. And in 1908 the Japanese Diet passed a bill requiring that middle school students be taught judo or kendo as a part of their education. This would have been a sweet victory for both of these pioneers.

Later in life (1909) Dr. Kano went on to become the first Japanese member of the International Olympic Committee. If that were not enough, in 1922 Dr. Kano was elected to the House of Peers. Unfortunately, he did not live to see his beloved judo become an official sport in the Olympics, as it did at the 1964 Tokyo Olympics.

If these men could have lived to see how their revival of this aspect of traditional Japanese culture has spread around the world, I am quite sure they would be surprised—but well pleased—with the results of their efforts.

Notes

1. Aus Uberzeugung tritt er den Germanen bei, die noch den burfchen gchaftlich großdeutfchen Traditionen huldigen.

Bibliography

Baelz, Toku, ed. *Awakening Japan: The Diary of a German Doctor: Erwin Baelz*. Bloomington, Indiana: Indiana University Press, 1974.

Bälz, Toku. *Erwin Bälz: Das Leben eines deutßchen Arztes im erwachenden Japan*. Stuttgart: J. Engelhorns Nachef. 1931.

Choi, H.H. *Taekwon-Do: The Art of Self-Defense*. Seoul, Korea: Daeha Publication Co., 1963.

Cott, J. *Wandering Ghost: The Odyssey of Lafcadio Hearn*. Tokyo: Kodansha International, 1990.

Drager, D.F. *The Martial Arts and Ways of Japan: Volume 1, Classical Bujutsu*. New York: Weatherhill, 1983.

———. *The Martial Arts and Ways of Japan: Volume 2, Classical Bujutsu*. New York: Weatherhill, 1975.

———. *The Martial Arts and Ways of Japan: Volume 3, Modern Bujutsu and Budo*. New York: Weatherhill, 1974.

Egami, S. *The Way of Karate: Beyond Technique*. Tokyo: Kodansha International, 1976.

Funakoshi, G. *Karate-Do Kyohan: The Master Text*. Tokyo: Kodansha International, 1973.

———. *Karate-Do: My Way of Life*. Tokyo: Kodansha International, 1975.

———. *Karate-Do Nyumon: The Master Introductory Text*. Tokyo: Kodansha International, 1988.

Haines, B.A. *Karate's History and Traditions*. Rutland, Vermont: Tuttle Publishing, 1968.

Hancock, H. Irving, and Katsukuma Higashi. *The Completed Kano Jiu-Jitsu (Jitso)*. New York: Dover Publications, Inc., 1961.

Hashimoto, Masae. *Atsukunai Okyu Nyumon (An Introduction to Acupuncture and Moxibusiton Without Cautery)*. Tokyo: Shufu to Seikatsusha, 1964.

Hisataka, M. *Scientific Karatedo*. Tokyo: Japan Publications, Inc., 1976.

Hooghe, Romein de. *Klare onderrichtinge der voortreffelijcke Worstel-konst*. Amsterdam: J. J. van Waesberge, 1674.

Hunter, H.H. *Super Ju-Jitsu: Vol. 1*. Ontario: Times Job Print, 1938.

———. *Super Ju-Jitsu: Vol. 2*. Ontario: Times Job Print, 1938.

James, A.A., et al. *Sports for Recreation and How to Play Them*. New York: A.S. Barnes and Company, 1946.

Khim, P.C., and D.F. Draeger. *Shaolin: An Introduction to Lohan Fighting Techniques*. Rutland, Vermont: Charles E. Tuttle Company, 1979.

Klinger-Klingerstorff, H. *Judo and Judo-Do*. London: Herbert Jenkins, 1953.

Kodokan. *Kodokan Judo: A Guide to Proficiency*. Tokyo: Kodansha International, 1963.

Koizumi, G. *My Study of Judo: The Principles and the Technical Fundamentals*. New York: Cornerstone Library, 1967.

Koyama, K., and A. Minami. *Jiu Jitsu: The Effective Japanese Mode of Self-Defense*. New York: American Sports Publishing, 1913.

Mason, R.H.P., and J.G. Caiger. *A History of Japan*. Rutland, Vermont: Tuttle Publishing, 1997.

Mattinson, J. *Stranger and Acquaintance Violence: Practice Messages from the British Crime Survey*. Briefing Note 7/01 (a publication of the Policing and Reducing Crime Unit), 2001.

McAleer, K. *Dueling: The Cult of Honor in Fin-de-siécle Germany*. Princeton: Princeton University Press, 1997.

McCarthy, P. *Ancient Okinawan Martial Arts: Loryu Uchinadi 2*. Rutland, Vermont: Charles Tuttle Co., 1999.

Metzner, H. *History of the American Turners*, 4th Revised Edition. Louisville, Kentucky: National Council of the American Turners, 1987.

Mitchell, D. *Skilled Defence*. Cleveland: Dewey Mitchell System of Skilled Defence, 1936.

Nagamine, S. *The Essence of Okinawan Karate-Do*. Rutland, Vermont: Charles E. Tuttle Company, 1985.

National Institute of Justice. *Use of Force by Police: Overview of National and Local Data*. Washington, DC: GPO, October 1999.

Nolte, C.E. The German Turnverien. 2001. Available at: http://cscwww.cats.ohiou.edu/~chastain/rz/turnvere.htm

Richie, D. *Lafacadio Hearn's Japan: An Anthology of His Writings on the Country and Its People*. Rutland, Vermont: Charles E. Tuttle Co., 1997.

Saito, M. *Aikido: Sword, Stick, and Body Arts: Vol. 1, 2, 3 & 4, Vital Techniques*. Tokyo: Minato Research, 1974.

Saito, M. *Aikido: Sword, Stick, and Body Arts: Vol. 4, Vital Techniques*. Tokyo: Minato Research, 1974.

Sasamori, J. and G. Warner. *This Is Kendo: The Art of Japanese Fencing*. Rutland, Vermont: Charles E. Tuttle Company, Inc., 1968.

Shioda, G. *Dynamic Aikido*. Tokyo: Kodansha: Tokyo, 1968.

Smith, R.W. *Secrets of Shaolin Temple Boxing*. Rutland, Vermont: Charles E. Tuttle Company, Inc., 1969.

Stevens, J. *Abundant Peace: The Biography of Morihei Ueshiba, Founder of Aikido*. Boston: Shambhala, 1987.

Stevens, J. *Three Budo Masters*. Tokyo: Kodansha International, 1995.

Tani, C. *Karate-Do*. Tani Karate Research Institute.

Tohei, K. *This Is Aikido*. Tokyo: Japan Publications, Inc., 1968.

Uyeshiba, K. *Aikido*. Tokyo: Kodansha International, 1962.

Vairamuttu, R.A. *Scientific Unarmed Combat: The Art of Dynamic Self-Defense and the Ancient Asian Pyscho-Physical Study*. London: W. Foulsham, 1954.

Wang, X. *64 Leg-Attack Methods of Shaoling Kungfu*. Hong Kong: Hai Feng Publishing Co., 1983.

Westbrook, A. and O. Ratti. *Aikido and the Dynamic Sphere: An Illustrated Introduction*. Rutland, Vermont: Charles E. Tuttle, 1970.

Yamada, Y. *Aikido Complete*. Sercauscus: Citadel Press, 1974.

Yamanaka, K. *Jiu-Jutsu*. Cleveland: Penton Press, 1918.